BRAIN
FOOD

BRAIN FOOD

Gemma Reece

Introduction by Judith Wills

Love Food ™ is an imprint of Parragon Books Ltd

Parragon
Queen Street House
4 Queen Street
Bath BA1 1HE, UK

ISBN: 978-1-4075-1877-0
Printed in Indonesia

Produced by the Bridgewater Book Company Ltd
Photographer: Clive Bozzard-Hill
Home economist: Sandra Baddeley

NOTES FOR THE READER
This book uses both imperial, metric or US cup measurements. Follow the same units of measurement throughout; do not mix imperial and metric. All spoon measurements are level: teaspoons are assumed to be 5 ml, and tablespoons are assumed to be 15 ml. Unless otherwise stated, milk is assumed to be whole, eggs and individual vegetables such as potatoes are medium, and pepper is freshly ground black pepper. Recipes using raw or very lightly cooked eggs should be avoided by infants, the elderly, pregnant women, convalescents, and anyone suffering from an illness. The times given are an approximate guide only.

PICTURE ACKNOWLEDGEMENTS
The publisher would like to thank the following for permission to reproduce copyright material: Corbis 7; Getty Images 14, 15, 16; iStock 9tl, 9br. Middle image on front cover by Corbis.

Judith Wills is a leading diet and nutrition expert. She is author of *The Food Bible*, *The Diet Bible*, and *The Children's Food Bible*, and co-author of *Feeding Kids*.
Her website is www.thedietdectective.net

Contents

Introduction

Can you really eat for a better brain?

The human brain is a powerful organ, but to work well it needs to be provided with good-quality fuel—a balanced diet containing a variety of important nutrients.

How does your brain work?

Your brain is the hub or powerhouse of the central nervous system. It is made up of about a 100 billion nerve cells, and each cell is connected to around 10,000 others. So the total number of connections (neurons) in your brain is approximately 1,000 trillion!

This remarkable control center enables you to think and make decisions. It also controls your body movements and processes, including speech, sight, hearing, and all the other senses. Ideas, planning, and emotions begin in the brain, and it is the source of memory and the ability to reason, communicate, and solve problems.

How does the right diet influence brainpower and functioning?

Your diet affects the brain chemicals that influence your mood, behavior, thought processes, learning ability, and reactions. Over the past 30 years or so—and especially in the past decade—scientists have been discovering more and more information about how what we eat affects the way our brain functions. We now know that a balanced diet—particularly one that is rich in certain important nutrients such as unsaturated fats, specific amino acids, and a variety of vitamins and other micronutrients—really does make a vital contribution to how well our brain works. And on the other hand, if we have a poor diet and lifestyle, brainpower may suffer as a result, both in the short and long term.

What nutrients does the brain need?

Because the brain is so complicated and has nonstop work to do, it is no wonder that it needs regular and adequate fuel. Its source of fuel is energy and nutrients from what you eat and drink—and five-star fuel will help it to work at optimum power, and with speed and fluidity.

● The brain's main source of fuel for energy is glucose. This arrives in the brain via the blood, which also supplies it with vital oxygen. The brain requires eight to ten times more glucose and oxygen than the body's other organs, as well as using 20 percent of the body's oxygen supply, even though it is only around 2 percent of our total weight. It needs this glucose and oxygen constantly, even as we sleep.

● Because around 60 percent of the solid matter of your brain is fat (and the working surfaces of your brain neurons are composed of thin layers of fat), you need fat in your diet. The types, amounts, and balance of fats that you eat can have a considerable effect on brainpower and health.

● Around 30 percent of solid brain matter is protein, made up of various amino acids that are mostly used to make and maintain the neurotransmitters (the neuron connectors), which they do with the help of certain vitamins and minerals, which are also of prime importance in the diet. The brain is approximately 77 percent water, and adequate fluid in the diet is also vital—3–4¼ pints (1.5–2 liters) a day.

Fats to feed your brain

It is true what our grandmothers used to say: fish really is good for the brain. The special omega-3 fatty acids DHA (docosahexaenoic acid) and EPA (eicosapentaenoic acid) that fish—particularly oily fish—contain (and which form a high percentage of the brain matter itself) are vital for brainpower. Researchers at Washington University believe that early modern humans had a high omega-3 diet of up to 50 percent fish and seafood, and that this is what enabled them to learn and evolve at such a fast rate.

Even today, these omega-3 fats (part of the polyunsaturated family of fats) are vital for brain health. They help development in the fetus and in childhood, and can help minimize or prevent brain diseases and problems in later life, such as poor memory or even Alzheimer's disease. Optimum intake of these fats can also, many research studies now seem to show, increase concentration, learning ability, and memory, as well as improve negative behavior.

The "parent" of the omega-3 group of fats is alpha-linolenic acid (ALA), one of the two "essential" fats in the diet. ALA is called essential because our bodies cannot manufacture it, so

Leafy greens

ABOVE AND RIGHT A variety of foods contain the types of fat which are good for the brain. While oily fish is one of the best sources of omega-3s, they can also be found in a variety of polyunsaturated nut and seed oils and in leafy greens and some shellfish. Avocados are a good source of mono-unsaturated oils, which are also healthy.

Best sources of omega-3 fats

Food per 3½ oz/100 g	Amount of EPA (mg)	DHA (mg)	Food per 3½ oz/100 g	Amount of omega-3 ALA (g)
FISH			**OIL**	
Halibut	526	393	Flaxseed oil	53
Herring/sardines, fresh	510	690	Hemp seed oil	19
Mackerel	710	1100	Flaxseeds	14
Salmon, fresh, farmed	618	1293	Walnut oil	11.5
Sardines, canned in oil	890	820	Rapeseed oil	9.6
Sea bass	161	434	Soya oil	7.3
Swordfish	108	531	Pumpkin seeds	7
Trout	230	830	Walnuts	5.6
Tuna, fresh	283	890	Dark leafy greens	1–2
SHELLFISH				
Crabmeat	470	450		
Mussels	410	160		

Crabs

Avocado

Pumpkin seeds

Oils

Oily fish

it has to be provided in what we eat and drink. The body can convert ALA into DHA and EPA (although this conversion is not always super-efficient) and so people who eat little or no fish, such as vegetarians, should ensure that their diets contain plenty of ALA (see box on page 8). Even people who do eat fish will benefit from the extra omega-3s that these foods provide.

How much omega-3 do we need? Nutritionists recommend that we all eat at least two portions of fish every week, one of which should be oily, which is equivalent to an average of 450 mg omega-3 (EPA/DHA). Total omega-3 intake (from all sources including plants) should be around 2 g (2,000 mg) a day, according to official guidelines.

The other branch of the polyunsaturated fats family is the omega-6s. The parent of this family is called linoleic acid and it is another essential fat. However, because it is present in

large amounts in many of the fats and oils that we choose today—such as corn oil, sunflower oil, safflower oil, and blended vegetable oils—many of us eat too much of this type of oil. It seems that a ratio between 5:1 and 2:1 may be ideal, whereas in the West, the ratio could be as high as 18:1. Experts now believe that it is the correct balance of omega-6s to omega-3s in the diet that can help us achieve and maintain good health.

A high intake of omega-6 fats—and saturated and trans fats—can block the good work of the omega-3s, so the ideal diet is one that supplies smaller amounts of omega-6s and higher amounts of omega-3s than we presently consume.

One good way of reducing the amount of omega-6s that we eat is to consume more monounsaturated fats (found in olive oil, rapeseed oil, peanut oil, walnut oil, or avocado) rather than highly polyunsaturated oils.

Other good brain nutrients

It is not just omega-3 fatty acids that can help feed the brain—a range of other nutrients have a significant role to play in helping brainpower and memory and protecting the brain from degeneration.

Antioxidants

Brain cells are especially vulnerable to attack by free radicals—molecular by-products of normal living that can be harmful in excess. These are "mopped up" and their production inhibited in the body by various compounds in the diet, which have been named "antioxidants." A high-antioxidant diet can significantly reduce the risk of cognitive loss—memory, judgement, and reasoning—and vitamin C can increase blood flow to the brain.

Some vitamins (such as C and E) and minerals (such as zinc and selenium) are powerful antioxidants, while many vegetables, fruits, and other plant foods contain antioxidant compounds, most of which have been analyzed and named only in recent years. Some of the plant chemicals with the strongest link to a healthy brain are the carotenoid group and the flavonoid group.

Choline

A vitamin-like component of the fatty acid lecithin, choline is used in our bodies to maintain cell membranes and transmit nerve impulses, and it is essential for optimum brain development in the young. It has also been claimed that choline may help prevent memory loss and improve cognitive function in older people. Traces of choline are found in many foods, but eggs are a particularly rich source of choline. Other sources include soybeans, cooked beef, chicken livers, and spinach.

L-tyrosine

L-tyrosine is an amino acid—a building block of protein. All the 22 amino acids are used to make the neurotransmitters (the neuron connectors) that enable your brain cells to communicate, but l-tyrosine is especially important for increasing alertness. As the brain consists of 8 percent protein as a whole, a diet reasonably high in protein is important. Foods such as lean meat, eggs, cheese, fish, poultry, and pulses are good high-protein foods.

Nutrient	Best sources	How much you need
ANTIOXIDANTS		
Vitamin C	Berry fruits, citrus fruits, kiwis, bell peppers, and green vegetables.	USA 75 mg/UK 40 mg/EC 60 mg.* Cannot be stored in the body, so needed daily.
Vitamin E	Olive oil, avocados, nuts, seeds and plant oils.	USA 15 mg/UK 5 mg/EC 10 mg.
Carotenoids	Carrots, red bell peppers, tomatoes, squashes, sweet potatoes, mangoes, and dark leafy greens.	No official RDAs for total carotenoids, but aim for 1–2 portions of orange or red plant food a day.
Flavonoids	Red and purple berries, grapes, olives, citrus fruits, onions, apples, leeks, garlic, fresh peas and beans, leafy greens, fresh herbs, and spices.	No official RDAs for flavonoids, but aim for 1 portion of flavonoid-rich food at every meal.
Choline	Eggs, wheatgerm, cabbage, peanuts, soybeans, sardines**, whole grains, peas, and beef.	No official RDAs for choline, but aim for 1–2 portions of choline-rich food a day.
L-tyrosine (protein)	Sharp hard cheese, milk, meat, oats, whole grains, avocados, almonds, and turkey.	No official RDAs for this specific amino acid, but total average requirement for adult male USA 56 g/UK 45 g; adult female USA 46 g/UK 36 g.

* USA and EC recommended daily amounts (RDAs) for vitamins and minerals are higher than those in the UK. ** For fish and sources of omega-3s, see page 8.

Nutrient	Best sources	How much you need
B VITAMINS		
Vitamin B1 (thiamine)	Whole grain and enriched-grain products such as fortified cereals, rice, pasta, and bread.	USA 1.1 mg (f); 1.2 mg (m)/UK 0.8 mg (f); 1 mg (m)/EC 1.4 mg.
Vitamin B6 (pyridoxine)	Found in chicken, fish, pork, liver, whole grain cereals, and nuts.	USA 1.3 mg./UK 1.2 mg (f); 1.4 mg (m)/EC 2 mg.
Folate (folic acid)	Found in fortified cereals, bananas, oranges, lemons, strawberries, leafy vegetables, and beans.	USA 400 ug./UK 200 ug/EC 200 ug.
Vitamin B12 (cyanocobalamin)	Found in eggs, milk and dairy products, meat, fish, and poultry.	USA 2.4 ug/UK 1.5 ug/EC 1 ug.
MINERALS		
Selenium	Seafood, Brazil nuts, lentils, whole wheat, and pork.	USA 55 ug/UK 60 ug/EC no RDA.
Magnesium	Nuts, whole grains, fresh peas and beans, green vegetables, and cocoa powder.	USA 320 mg (f); 420 mg (m)/UK 270 mg/EC 300 mg.
Zinc	Shellfish, nuts and seeds, whole grains, lean red meat, and sharp hard cheese.	USA 8 mg (f); 11 mg (m)/UK 7 mg (f); 9.5 mg (m)/ EC 15 mg.
Iron	Red meat, beans, leafy greens, whole grains, seeds, dried fruit, and eggs.	USA 18 mg (f); 8 mg (m)/UK 14.8 mg (f); 8.7 mg (m)/EC 14 mg.
LOW GI FOODS	Beans, oats, rye, pasta, fruit, whole grain breads, yogurt, and green vegetables.	Aim to choose low-GI foods at every meal.

B vitamins

The vitamin B group is vital for brain function.

Vitamin B1 (thiamine) helps to release energy from carbohydrates for a healthy brain and nerve cells. It is found in whole grain and enriched-grain products.

Vitamin B6 (pyridoxine) is vital for the metabolism of l-tyrosine and the other amino acids.

Folate (folic acid) is vital for fatty acid and amino acid metabolism in the brain and prevention of neural tube defects in unborn babies.

Vitamin B12 (cyanocobalamin) is vital for healthy nervous tissue, converting carbohydrates into brain energy, metabolizing essential fats for the brain, and helping build and maintain healthy nerve cells.

Minerals

Important minerals include: selenium, which helps the work of vitamin E; magnesium, an aid to the smooth running of the brain; and iron, vital for transporting oxygen to the brain.

Other factors

Regular eating is important to provide the constant glucose supply that your brain needs. A diet containing plenty of low-glycemic index (GI) foods will help, as these are less quickly absorbed by the bloodstream and help to keep blood sugar levels constant. Breakfast is a vital meal of the day for brain functioning after the long night's fast.

What not to eat

Some foods can have a negative effect on the brain. A diet high in saturated and trans fats (such as full-fat dairy produce, fatty cuts of meat, pastry, cookies, cakes, processed desserts, and chips) can block the work of the "good" omega-3 fatty acids, and so it is important to try to cut right back on these in your diet. A high intake of alcohol is also linked with brain degeneration, and a typical "junk food" diet will probably not contain all the nutrients your brain needs for good health.

Brain foods for life

Throughout your life, what you eat can help your brain to function well. The following offers an insight into how brain foods can affect different life stages.

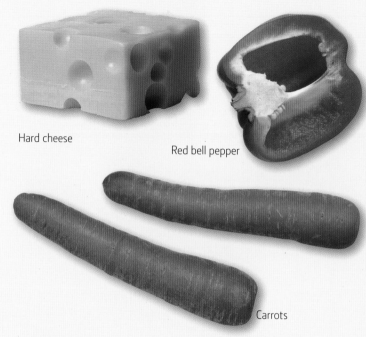

Hard cheese

Red bell pepper

Carrots

Before birth, and infancy

While a baby is in the womb, his or her brain grows more rapidly than in any other stage of infant or child development, and faster than any other part of the body. During the first year after birth, the brain continues to grow rapidly, tripling in size by an infant's first birthday.

• Neural tube defects (NTDs) of the spinal chord and brain are one of the most common birth defects and can be prevented by adequate folate (folic acid) in the mother's diet.

• High alcohol consumption during pregnancy can increase the risk of hyperactivity, attention deficiency, and emotional problems in children.

• Research on a large group of pregnant women, published in *The Lancet* in 2007, has found that low omega-3 diets during pregnancy can result in children with suboptimal brain development and with reduced verbal IQ.

• Some researchers have also found that low omega-3 diets during pregnancy can result in children who experience increased behavioral problems.

• Research on animals published in the *New Scientist* in 2004 found that extra choline in the diet while a woman is pregnant may improve her child's brainpower.

• Infants who have low amounts of DHA in their diet have reduced brain development and diminished visual clarity.

• The increased intelligence and academic performance of breastfed compared with formula-fed infants may be attributed in part to the higher DHA content of human milk.

Childhood

A variety of scientific trials show that children who eat an optimum range of nutrients have improved IQ, concentration, and memory.

• Research in 2005 on children aged between 5 and 12 has shown that a regular intake of omega-3 oils can have a significant impact upon learning, attention, memory, reading ability, and behavior. Some children improved by as much as four academic years in a six-month trial. While the research is carried out using supplements, it is reasonable to assume that a diet high in foods naturally rich in omega-3s would have a similar effect.

• A balanced, nutrient-rich breakfast is a vital meal of the day for kids. Several research trials have found that those who have only high-sugar, high-GI drinks or foods at breakfast—or no breakfast at all—perform significantly less well at tasks requiring concentration, memory, and alertness.

• The right diet plays an important role in helping older children and teenagers both to revise for and to perform more effectively during exams.

Tomatoes

Eggs

Oranges

LEFT Hard cheese is an excellent source of l-tyrosine, which can help improve alertness and memory as we age. Red bell peppers and carrots are both excellent sources of antioxidant carotenoids, while bell peppers are also rich in vitamin C, another antioxidant. These can help improve cognitive power.

ABOVE Tomatoes are rich in both carotenoids and vitamin C—the deeper the colors, the more carotene they contain. Eggs are one of the best sources of choline, which is essential for brain development in the young. Oranges are high in vitamin C and flavonoids, which help blood flow to the brain and mop up "free radicals" that can harm the brain.

• The long-chain omega-6 fatty acid GLA (gamma-linoleic acid), found in evening primrose and starflower oils, may also help children's brain function.

• Fish oil and evening primrose oil can also help to combat the problems of dyslexia and ADHD (attention deficit hyperactivity disorder).

Adulthood

As we get older and face the normal stresses and problems of everyday life, a balanced diet containing adequate omega-3 and other "brain foods" can help us to maintain brainpower. It can also help avoid problems such as loss of memory, Alzheimer's disease, and depression.

• L-tyrosine becomes depleted when we are under stress and supplementing with l-tyrosine-rich foods (see page 10) may improve alertness and memory.

• An overview of international studies, conducted by the National Institutes of Health, USA, found that pregnant women with diets low in omega-6s have an increased risk of suffering from depression.

Old age

Even into old age, brain foods can help keep us alert and ward off fading memory and other typical problems such as lack of concentration and mental stamina.

• In a study published in *Psychosomatic Medicine* in 2007, older adults who had diets high in omega-6 fatty acids and low in omega-3 fatty acids appeared to be more prone to depression and stress.

• According to research carried out in 2006 by the Department of Psychological and Brain Sciences, Duke University, North Carolina, low levels of choline are associated with Alzheimer's disease, and boosting dietary intake (see page 10) may slow memory loss in old age.

• Research carried out on aging dogs has shown that a high intake of antioxidant-rich foods can improve cognitive skills.

• It is vital to keep a healthy blood flow to the brain as we age and a diet rich in omega-3s and antioxidants, plus regular exercise, is probably a major key to healthy circulation and continuing brain health.

Brain foods for children

Knowing what to feed your children for good brain health is one thing, but getting them to eat it is quite another. However, changes can be successfully achieved by following these simple tips.

● Children's diet begins with what you buy at the supermarket. Don't be swayed in your choices.

● Encourage your children to be interested in what they eat and why good food is important for them. Most small children love helping with food in the kitchen and most will try items such as vegetables if they have helped to shop for or prepare them.

● Sometimes fussy and poor eaters eat better when the portions are small—they can be discouraged when faced with a large plateful. Over time you can increase the amounts. Toddlers and small children often eat better when offered finger foods.

● Serve only one new food at a time, offer a very small amount, and serve a new food with a familiar food.

● Let children develop a good natural appetite for their meals by avoiding giving them large between-meal snacks or high-calorie drinks. Do not give them any snacks in the hour before mealtime.

Tips for increasing brain food intake
Vegetables

● If you have a garden, let your children cultivate some quick-growing lettuce and radish—growing their own will encourage them to eat salad items.

● Prepare vegetables in a cheese sauce and/or with pasta and/or in a casserole.

● Blend vegetables into smooth soups or add very small chunks to a meat or chicken casserole.

● Overcooked and soggy vegetables are a discouragement for most children—stir-frying or baking are more appealing ways to cook them.

● Children often enjoy crunching on crisp, raw fresh vegetables cut into strips to be eaten with fingers—with a tasty dip, perhaps.

● Serve a very finely chopped or puréed vegetable sauce with pasta, rice, or a baked potato.

Fish

● Almost all children love fish nuggets, cakes, or fingers, and they are all very easy—and healthier—to make at home (see Real Fish Nuggets on page 71).

● Most children love a cheesy tuna casserole. Try a lowfat cheese sauce for a healthier option. Fish kabobs threaded with cherry tomatoes are another good idea.

● To encourage children to eat more oily fish, try salmon fish fingers or make a pasta dish with salmon or fresh tuna flakes. Salmon or tuna pâté is easy to make and an ideal sandwich filler.

Swap to brain food

- Swap a bag of chips for a small handful of almonds, Brazil nuts, or cashew nuts (for children aged over five years).

- Swap a pack of candies or a chocolate bar for a small bag you have made up yourself containing a few chocolate chips, a few pieces of dried fruit, and a few nuts.

- Swap a slice of white bread and jam for a rice cake topped with a little nut butter (butter blended with ground nuts).

- Swap a slice of sponge cake for one of the brain-friendly snacks in the Breakfasts and Treats section.

Lunch boxes

An ideal pack lunch will contain a balance of nutrients—some protein, good-quality carbohydrate, some fat, and a range of vitamins and minerals, including some vitamin C.
The ideal drink is water—occasionally milk or diluted whole fruit juice are fine. Whole juice is better for blood sugars, and is less likely to contribute to tooth decay.

Five complete lunch-box meals

The following meals are for children aged 5 years or more:

1 Sandwich of whole wheat bread filled with tuna mashed with plain yogurt and lemon juice; 3 cherry tomatoes; 1 small apple; 1 slice of Carrot Cake.

2 1 whole wheat pita bread filled with hummus and a selection of chopped vegetables; 1 individual pot of plain yogurt with honey; 1 Oatmeal, Apple, and Cinnamon Muffin; 1 small orange.

3 1 box of homemade pasta salad with chicken or cheddar cheese, chopped red bell pepper, cucumber, red onion, pumpkin seeds, and olive oil and lemon dressing; 1 slice of rich fruit cake; 1 plum.

4 Whole wheat roll filled with hard-cooked egg, tomato, and watercress; handful of red grapes; 1 slice of Walnut and Banana Cake; 1 individual pot of lowfat plain yogurt.

Brain food recipes

This book contains a section of recipes specifically aimed at children, but most of the recipes in the other sections are also highly suitable for children—the symbol © means "suitable for children" and, if necessary, a minimum age is given in addition. Always check that your child is older than the minimum age stated if serving the dish to them.

Other recipes in this book that are likely to appeal to most children are:

- Tomato, Lentil, and Red Bell Pepper Soup
- Creamy Salmon Baked Potatoes
- Tuna Steaks with Catalan Sauce
- Fish and Filo Pie
- Salmon Potato Patties with Jalapeño (use mild chiles)
- Spicy Shrimp with Cashew Nuts
- Traditional Spanish Frittata with Herb Salad
- Ratatouille with Poached Eggs (only for children aged over 5 because of the lightly cooked egg)
- Sweet Chili Chicken with Creole Rice
- Lamb Kabobs with Greek Salad
- Spicy Chicken with Tortilla Wrap
- Hoisin Beef with Mushrooms
- Any of the recipes in the Breakfasts and Treats section.

5 Sandwich of whole wheat bread filled with salmon mashed with wheat, cucumber, and scallion slices; carrot batons; 1 small pack of dried mixed fruit or golden raisins.

Add a drink of water to every box for vital hydration.

Eating plans

A balanced and nutritious diet for the brain isn't simply about individual nutrients or foods—you need a variety of foods each day to ensure that you really do eat to improve brainpower.

Each plan contains a selection of recipes from this book, as well as several non-recipe meals. Each day's eating not only provides high levels of the important "brain foods" mentioned in this chapter, but also gives a balanced and healthy diet overall, high in fruits and vegetables and reasonably low in sodium and low in so-called "junk" foods. Don't forget to drink adequate fluid. Aim for approximately 3–4¹/₄ pints (1.5–2 liters) a day—water is ideal.

Children's Eating Plan

BREAKFAST	LUNCH	SUPPER
Monday Oatmeal made with lowfat milk and a handful of mixed dried fruit added, 1 small orange.	Packed lunch (see page 15) or low-salt, low-sugar Boston beans on whole wheat toast topped with 1 tablespoon grated sharp cheddar cheese. 1 apple	Salmon Fish Cakes with peas and broiled tomato. 1 individual pot of lowfat fruit yogurt
Tuesday 1 slice of whole wheat toast with smooth peanut butter (aged over 1 year). 1 individual pot of lowfat fruit yogurt, 1 plum	Packed lunch (see page 15) or poached egg (soft-poached only for children aged 3 years or more) on whole wheat toast. 1 orange	Butternut and Bean Casserole. Broccoli
Wednesday Whole grain cereal with lowfat milk and a handful of fresh berries. 1 slice of whole wheat toast with lowfat peanut butter	Packed lunch (see page 15) or cooked chicken breast slices tossed with chopped raw vegetables and cooked brown rice	Thin-crust Vegetable Pizza. Mixed-leaf side salad. 1 pear or nectarine
Thursday Lowfat plain yogurt topped with Fresh Fruit Salad with Blueberries and a handful of any whole grain cereal	Packed lunch (see page 15) or Tomato, Lentil, and Red Bell Pepper Soup. 1 whole wheat roll. 1 individual pot of lowfat yogurt	Tuna Pasta Casserole. Mixed-leaf side salad. 1 apple
Friday As Monday	Packed lunch (see page 15) or hummus, whole wheat pita bread and chopped salad. 1 individual pot of lowfat fruit yogurt	Meatballs with Tomato Sauce. Brown rice. snow peas

BREAKFAST	LUNCH	SUPPER
Saturday Yogurt and Strawberry Smoothie. 2 rye crispbreads	Creamy Salmon Baked Potato. Baked tomatoes.	Veggie Burger served with fries and peas or low-salt, low-sugar Boston beans. 1 small orange
Sunday 1–2 hard-cooked eggs. 1–2 slices of whole wheat bread. 1 orange	Chunky Sweet Potato and Lima Bean Soup. 1 individual pot of lowfat fruit yoghurt.	Lean roast beef, new potatos, dark green cabbage, carrots, peas. Fresh Fruit Salad with Blueberries topped with Oat and Nut Crunch Mix and lowfat plain yoghurt.

Adults' Eating Plan

Monday Muesli topped with blueberries and skimmed milk	Avocado and walnut salad with dark salad greens and olive oil dressing. 1 slice of Walnut and Seed Bread. 1 apple	Lamb Steaks with Tomatoes. Steamed broccoli
Tuesday Oatmeal made with water and skimmed milk sprinkled with pumpkin seeds. $\frac{1}{2}$ pink grapefruit	Quick and Spicy Pâté with Tuna. 2–3 rye crispbread. Watercress and cherry tomatoes	Sweet Chili Chicken with Creole Rice. Mixed-greens side salad. Fresh Fruit Salad with Blueberries
Wednesday 1 Oatmeal, Apple, and Cinnamon Muffin. 1 individual pot of lowfat yogurt. 1 orange	Couscous, Nut, and Chickpea Pilaf. Handful of red grapes.	Baked Sea Bass with White Bean Purée. Steamed green beans and snow peas.
Thursday Yogurt and Strawberry Smoothie	Tuna, Lentil, and Potato Salad. Handful of red grapes	Red Bell Pepper Falafel with Hummus Dressing. Whole wheat pasta shapes. Arugula and spinach salad
Friday As Monday	Spicy Chicken with Tortilla Wrap. 1 apple	Traditional Spanish Tortilla with Herb Salad. 1 orange
Saturday 1 individual pot of lowfat plain yogurt topped with Fresh Fruit Salad with Blueberries and a handful of Oat and Nut Crunch Mix	Ribollito (Tuscan Bean Soup)	Hoisin Beef with Mushrooms. Brown basmati rice
Sunday 1–2 hard-cooked eggs. 1–2 slices of whole bread. 1 orange	Chunky Sweet Potato and Lima Bean Soup. 1 individual pot of lowfat fruit yoghurt.	Lean roast beef, new potatos, dark green cabbage, carrots, peas. Fresh Fruit Salad with Blueberries topped with Oat and Nut Crunch Mix and lowfat plain yoghurt.

Soups, Salads, and Snacks

Within this chapter you will find plenty of healthy ideas for quick and easy lunches and suppers, whatever the time of year. Soups are ideal for getting plenty of vegetables and beans into your diet, while salads and snacks can be a great way to eat carbohydrates, protein, vegetables, nuts, and seeds.

KEY
Ⓥ Suitable for vegetarians
Ⓓ Ideal for weight control
Ⓟ Suitable for pregnancy
Ⓒ Suitable for children
Ⓠ Quick to prepare and cook
Ⓛ Low cost

Tomato, Lentil, and Red Bell Pepper Soup

> **NUTRITION NOTES** This soup is rich in carotenes, vitamin C, and vitamin E, all antioxidants that are vital for the healthy oxygenation of the brain and to protect against free radicals. Lentils are rich in iron to help memory and learning power, and also in selenium, which works with vitamin E to increase the beneficial effects of both.

SERVES 4 Ⓥ Ⓓ Ⓟ Ⓒ Ⓛ

3 tbsp olive oil

2 onions, chopped

2 garlic cloves, chopped

2 large red bell peppers, seeded and chopped

1 lb 2 oz /500 g ripe tomatoes, chopped

$^1/_2$ cup red lentils

2 $^1/_2$ cups vegetable stock, plus extra for thinning (optional)

1 tbsp red wine vinegar

salt and pepper

2 scallions, chopped, or 1 tbsp snipped fresh chives, for garnish

1 Heat the oil in a large skillet over medium-high heat, then add the onions and cook, stirring, for 5 minutes, or until softened but not browned. Add the garlic and red bell peppers and cook, stirring, for 5 minutes, or until the red bell peppers are softened.

2 Add the tomatoes, lentils, and stock and bring to a simmer. Reduce the heat to low, then cover and simmer gently for 25 minutes, or until the lentils are tender. Stir in the vinegar and season with a little salt and pepper to taste.

3 Let cool slightly, then transfer the soup to a blender or food processor and blend for 1 minute, or until smooth. Return to the skillet and reheat, stirring in a little hot water or stock if the soup seems a little too thick.

4 Serve in warmed bowls, garnished with the scallions.

Cook's Tip
* This soup is also good served cold.

Ribollito (Tuscan Bean Soup)

> **NUTRITION NOTES** This soup is packed with brain-friendly nutrients, including protein, vitamin C, magnesium, choline, carotene, lutein, vitamin E, and omega-3 fatty acids.

SERVES 4–6 Ⓥ Ⓓ Ⓟ Ⓒ Ⓛ

2 tbsp olive oil

1 large red onion, sliced

2 celery stalks, chopped

1 large carrot, coarsely chopped

2 large garlic cloves, chopped

14 oz/400 g canned chopped tomatoes with herbs

14 oz /400 g canned cannellini or borlotti beans, drained and rinsed

9 oz /250 g cavolo nero (Italian black cabbage), kale, or Savoy cabbage

2 $^1/_2$ cups vegetable or chicken stock

1 $^1/_2$ cups stale white or whole wheat breadcrumbs

2 tbsp chopped fresh flat-leaf parsley

salt and pepper

1 Heat the oil in a large saucepan over medium heat, then add the onion, celery, carrot, and garlic and cook, stirring frequently, for 8–10 minutes, or until softened.

2 Add the tomatoes and their juice, beans, cavolo nero, and stock, then stir well and bring to a simmer. Crush some of the beans against the side of the saucepan to help thicken the soup. Cover and cook over a low heat for 45 minutes–1 hour, or until all the vegetables are tender. Season with a little salt and pepper to taste. If you have time, let the soup stand for a few hours to thicken up and for the flavors to develop.

3 Sprinkle the breadcrumbs and parsley over the soup 30 minutes before you are ready to serve and reheat, uncovered, over low heat (or see Cook's Tip). The soup should be quite thick, with not much liquid remaining.

4 Spoon into warmed bowls to serve.

Cook's Tip
* You can cook the soup in a flameproof casserole, then, for Step 3, transfer to a preheated oven at 375°F/190°C and cook, uncovered, for 30 minutes to brown the breadcrumbs lightly.

Gado Gado (Indonesian Warm Salad)

NUTRITION NOTES This salad is a great source of choline, carotene, iron, and vitamins C and E.

SERVES 4 Ⓥ Ⓟ Ⓒ (aged over 1 year), Ⓛ

8 outer leaves of romaine lettuce or similar dark, crisp lettuce leaves

3¹/₂ oz/100 g green beans, lightly cooked

3¹/₂ oz/100 g baby carrots, lightly cooked

9 oz/250 g salad new potatoes, such as Charlotte, cooked until just tender

1 tbsp peanut oil

generous ³/₄ cup fresh bean sprouts

3¹/₄-inch/8-cm piece cucumber, seeded and cut into 1¹/₂-inch/4-cm batons

4 eggs, hard-cooked

1 small mild onion, sliced into rings

SAUCE

4 tbsp canned reduced-fat coconut milk

3 tbsp sugar-free smooth peanut butter

juice of ¹/₂ lime

2 tsp light soy sauce

dash of Tabasco sauce or any chili sauce

1 Roughly tear the lettuce leaves, if large, and arrange on 4 individual serving plates or 1 large serving platter. Halve the beans and cut the carrots, as necessary, into batons. Arrange these with the potatoes (cut into chunks if large) on the plates or platter.

2 Heat the oil in a nonstick skillet or wok over high heat, then add the bean sprouts and stir-fry for 2 minutes, or until lightly cooked or still crisp. Remove with a slotted spoon and sprinkle over the cooked vegetables with the cucumber. Peel and quarter the eggs, then arrange on top of the salad.

3 Add the onion rings to the oil remaining in the skillet or wok and stir-fry over high heat for 5 minutes, or until golden and crisp. Combine all the ingredients for the sauce in a small bowl and pour over the salad. Top with the onion rings and serve immediately.

Cook's Tips

* This dish is best served when all the cooked vegetables are still warm. It is a superb special-occasion main course salad for vegetarians.

* To save time, you could buy ready-made peanut (satay) sauce and thin it with a little canned reduced-fat coconut milk.

* For diners over 5 years old, you can sprinkle chopped peanuts and/or sesame seeds over the top for garnish.

Chunky Sweet Potato and Lima Bean Soup

NUTRITION NOTES Orange-fleshed sweet potatoes are a brilliant source of vitamins A, C, and E—powerful antioxidants—while beans are a good source of choline and folate.

SERVES 4 Ⓥ Ⓓ Ⓟ Ⓒ Ⓠ Ⓛ

2 tbsp olive oil

1 onion, chopped

2 celery stalks, chopped

1 large carrot, coarsely chopped

1 large or 2 small sweet potatoes, peeled and chopped

14 oz/400 g canned lima beans or cannellini beans, drained and rinsed

4 cups vegetable stock

1 large handful fresh cilantro leaves

2 tbsp freshly grated Parmesan cheese

salt and pepper

1 Heat the oil in a large saucepan over medium heat, then add the onion, celery, and carrot and cook, stirring frequently, for 8–10 minutes, or until softened. Add the sweet potatoes and beans and cook, stirring, for 1 minute.

2 Add the stock, then stir thoroughly and bring to a simmer. Season with a little salt and pepper to taste. Cover, then reduce the heat and cook for 25–30 minutes, or until all the vegetables are tender.

3 Let cool slightly, then transfer one-third of the soup to a blender or food processor and blend until smooth. Return to the saucepan and mix in well. Check the seasoning and reheat.

4 Ladle into warmed bowls and scatter with the cilantro and Parmesan cheese before serving.

Variations

* You can blend all the soup for a change, to make a smooth vegetable soup.
* You can use dried beans in any recipe that features canned beans—follow the package directions for preparing and cooking; many require presoaking overnight and lengthy cooking times.

Italian Fish Soup
with White Wine

NUTRITION NOTES This fish soup is a good source of omega-3 fatty acids, selenium, and zinc, and contains vegetables rich in antioxidants for a healthy brain.

SERVES 4 ⒟ ⒫ Ⓒ (aged over 5 years), ⒬

4 tbsp olive oil

3 leeks, sliced

2 celery stalks, chopped

1 large onion, chopped

2 large garlic cloves, well crushed

9 oz/250 g cremini mushrooms, sliced

4 cups fish stock

9 oz/250 g canned tomatoes

scant ¹/₂ cup Italian dry white wine

1 tsp hot paprika

1 lb/450 g mixed fish fillets, such as cod, sea bass, monkfish, red
  snapper, and sea bream, cut into bite-size pieces

1 lb/450 g mixed raw seafood, such as shrimp in their shells, cleaned
  mussels in their shells, cleaned squid, cut into rings and tentacles
  chopped, and crabmeat (cooked), including claws

salt and pepper

plenty of chopped fresh flat-leaf parsley, for garnish

1 Heat the oil in a large saucepan or flameproof casserole over medium heat. Add the leeks, celery, onion, and garlic and cook, stirring frequently, for 8–10 minutes, or until softened. Add the mushrooms, stock, tomatoes and their juice, and wine and stir well.

2 Bring to a simmer and add the paprika and a little salt and pepper to taste. Then add all the fish and seafood and simmer gently for 15 minutes. Check the seasoning.

3 Serve in warmed bowls, garnished with the parsley.

Cook's Tips

* Clean mussels by scrubbing or scraping the shells and pulling out any beards attached to the mussels. Discard any opened mussels or mussels with broken shells. Discard closed mussels after cooking.
* Shellfish is one of the foods likely to cause an allergic reaction in children, but non-allergic children can eat this soup, or you could substitute other fish for the shellfish.

Tuna, Lentil, and Potato Salad

NUTRITION NOTES This soup is high in omega-3 fatty acids, vitamin B6, folate, and vitamin E.

SERVES 4 ℗ © ℚ

1 cup Puy or brown lentils

2 tbsp olive oil, plus extra for brushing

10¹/₂ oz/300 g baby new potatoes, washed

1 head Boston lettuce

4 fresh tuna steaks, about 3¹/₂ oz/100 g each

12 small cherry tomatoes, halved

1¹/₂ oz/40 g arugula leaves

salt and pepper

DRESSING

5 tbsp fruity olive oil

1 tbsp balsamic vinegar

2 tsp red wine vinegar

1 tsp smooth Dijon mustard

1 tsp soft light brown sugar

1 Cook the lentils in a saucepan of boiling water for 25 minutes, or until tender. Drain, then tip into a bowl and stir in the oil.

2 Meanwhile, cook the potatoes in a separate saucepan of lightly salted water for 15 minutes, or until just tender.

3 Break off the outer lettuce leaves and cut the heart into 8 evenly sized pieces. Arrange on 4 individual serving plates.

4 Put all the ingredients for the dressing, with a little salt and pepper to taste, in a screw-top jar and shake well to combine.

5 When the potatoes are nearly cooked, lightly brush a ridged broiler pan with oil and heat over high heat. When very hot, add the tuna steaks and cook for 1¹/₂ minutes on each side to sear. Remove to a cutting board and cut each steak into 6 chunks.

6 Drain the potatoes and coarsely chop any larger ones. Arrange with the lentils, tuna, and tomatoes on the serving plates, then sprinkle over the arugula leaves and spoon over the dressing. Serve immediately.

Cook's Tips
* If you don't have a broiler pan, you can cook the tuna steaks in a nonstick skillet lightly brushed with olive oil.
* To save time, you can make a large batch of the dressing in a screw-top jar—it will keep for several weeks in the refrigerator. Set aside at room temperature for 1 hour and shake well before using.

Rice, Salmon, and Pesto Salad

NUTRITION NOTES This salad is a good source of omega-3 fatty acids, vitamin E, magnesium, iron, and zinc.

SERVES 4 Ⓟ Ⓒ (aged over 5 years), Ⓠ Ⓛ

1 ¼ cups brown basmati rice
3 garlic cloves, peeled
1 tsp sea salt
1 large handful fresh basil sprigs
5 tbsp olive oil, plus extra for drizzling
²/₃ cup pine nuts
14 oz /400 g skinless salmon fillets
pepper

1 Cook the rice according to the package directions using the absorption method—with standard brown basmati rice, this should take around 30 minutes. Once tender, leave the rice in the saucepan, covered, off the heat.

2 Meanwhile, to make the pesto, put the garlic cloves and salt in a mortar and thoroughly crush with a pestle. Remove the stalks from the basil and add three-quarters of the basil leaves to the mortar with 2 tablespoons of the oil. Crush again, then add half the pine nuts with a further 2 tablespoons of the remaining oil and pepper to taste. Pound again until you have a thick paste.

3 Heat the remaining 1 tablespoon of oil in a large, nonstick skillet over high heat. When hot, add the salmon fillets and cook for 1½ minutes on each side to sear. Reduce the heat and cook for an additional 1–2 minutes, or until the fish is done to your liking (don't overcook), adding the remaining pine nuts to the skillet to cook, stirring, until golden. Remove the salmon and pine nuts from the skillet. Flake the salmon flesh into large pieces.

4 Lightly combine the rice, salmon flakes, and pesto in a salad bowl. Top with the remaining basil leaves, the toasted pine nuts, and a drizzle of oil.

Cook's Tip
* You can use white basmati rice if you prefer, but you will lose B vitamins.

Couscous, Nut, and Chickpea Pilaf

NUTRITION NOTES This dish is a good source of l-tyrosine, iron, vitamin B6, folate, omega-3 fatty acids, selenium, vitamin E, and zinc.

SERVES 4 Ⓥ Ⓓ Ⓟ Ⓒ (aged over 5 years), Ⓠ Ⓛ

7 oz/200 g quick-cook couscous (see Cook's Tips)
1 ½ cups vegetable stock
1 large yellow bell pepper, seeded and chopped
4 scallions, chopped
10 dried apricots, chopped
scant ¹/₃ cup golden raisins
½ cup slivered almonds, toasted
½ cup walnut pieces
1 heaped tablespoon pumpkin seeds
5½ oz/150 g drained, canned chickpeas, rinsed
2 tbsp pumpkin seed oil

1 Put the couscous in a large, heatproof bowl. Heat the stock in a saucepan to boiling point, then pour over the couscous and stir well. Cover and let stand for 15 minutes, by which time all the liquid should have been absorbed.

2 Stir all the remaining ingredients, except the oil, into the couscous, forking through lightly. Serve drizzled with the oil.

Cook's Tips
* This recipe uses quick-cook couscous, but if you have more time, you can buy traditional couscous (from health-food stores), which contains more iron and B vitamins. Follow the package directions to prepare.
* Pumpkin seed oil makes a tasty change from olive oil, is high in omega-3 fatty acids, and is now widely available.

Variation
* You can use whatever nuts and seeds you like—try cashew nuts, pine nuts, or sunflower seeds.

Easy Bean Dip with Crudités

NUTRITION NOTES This pâté is a good source of vitamins B1, B6, B12, C and E, carotene, iron, and zinc.

SERVES 4 ⓋⒹⓅⒸ (aged over 1 year), ⓆⓁ

14 oz/400 g canned cannellini beans, drained and rinsed
5¹/₂ oz/150 g strained plain yogurt
1 large garlic clove, well crushed
1 heaped tbsp sun-dried tomato paste
1 bottled or canned red bell pepper, drained and chopped
selection of crudités, such as carrots, celery, bell peppers, onion, and
 cucumber, cut into batons or strips, and/or lettuce hearts, leaves
 separated, and lightly cooked asparagus tips or baby corn, cooled,
 about 1 lb 2 oz/500 g in total
salt and pepper

1 Put all the ingredients, except the crudités, in a blender or food processor and blend for 1 minute. Spoon into a bowl, then cover and chill in the refrigerator for 30 minutes.

2 Meanwhile, prepare the crudités. Arrange on a platter and serve with the chilled dip.

Cook's Tip
* Use half the yogurt mixture to make a delicious pâté or sandwich filling instead of a dip.

Variations
* You can use lima beans in place of the cannellini beans.

Creamy Salmon Baked Potatoes

NUTRITION NOTES This potato dish is a good source of omega-3 fatty acids and vitamins B6, B12, C, and E.

SERVES 4 ⒹⓅⒸⓆⓁ

4 baking potatoes, about 9³/₄ oz/275 g each, scrubbed
9 oz/250 g skinless salmon fillet
7 oz/200 g lowfat soft cheese
2–3 tbsp skim milk
2 tbsp chopped/snipped fresh herbs, such as dill or chives
generous ¹/₂ cup grated, sharp cheddar cheese
salt and pepper

1 Preheat the oven to 400°F/200°C. Prick the skins of the potatoes and put on the top shelf of the preheated oven. Bake for 50–60 minutes, or until the skins are crisp and the centers are soft when pierced with a sharp knife or skewer.

2 Meanwhile, lightly poach the salmon fillet in a saucepan of gently simmering water for 4–5 minutes (if in one piece), or until just cooked but still moist. Alternatively, cut into 2–3 evenly sized pieces and cook in a microwave oven on medium heat for 2 minutes, then turn the pieces around so that the cooked parts are in the center, and cook for an additional 1 minute, or until just cooked but still moist. Using a fork, flake the flesh into a bowl.

3 In a separate bowl, blend the soft cheese with just enough of the milk to loosen, then stir in the herbs and a little salt and pepper.

4 When the potatoes are cooked, preheat the broiler to high. Cut the potatoes in half lengthwise. Carefully scoop the potato flesh out of the skins, reserving the skins, then add to the soft cheese mixture and mash together. Lightly stir in the salmon flakes.

5 Spoon the filling into the potato skins and top with the cheddar cheese. Cook under the preheated broiler for 1–2 minutes, or until the cheese is bubbling and turning golden. Serve immediately.

Cook's Tip
* Pregnant women should avoid using unpasteurized cream cheese or mold-ripened cheeses such as Brie in this recipe.

Eggs and Bell Peppers on Toast

> **NUTRITION NOTES** This dish is an excellent source of choline, vitamins B12, E, and folate, and also a good source of vitamins B6, C, and E, and carotene.

SERVES 4 Ⓓ Ⓟ Ⓒ (see Cook's Tips), Ⓠ Ⓛ

2 tbsp olive oil
2 large red bell peppers, seeded and chopped
1 small red onion, very finely chopped
pinch of paprika, plus extra for garnish (optional)
4 slices dark rye bread
8 large organic eggs
4 tbsp skim milk
salt and pepper

1 Heat half the oil in a nonstick skillet over medium-high heat, then add the red bell peppers and onion and cook, stirring frequently, for 10 minutes, or until soft. Add the paprika, then stir and set aside.

2 Toast one side of the bread slices. Brush the other sides with 1 tablespoon of the remaining oil, then lightly toast. Keep warm.

3 Beat the eggs with the milk and a little salt and pepper to taste in a bowl. Brush the remaining oil over the bottom of a nonstick saucepan, then add the egg mixture and cook over medium-high heat, stirring frequently to make sure that the eggs don't stick, for 5 minutes, or until cooked to your liking.

4 Gently stir in the red bell pepper mixture, then spoon onto the rye toasts. Sprinkle with a little extra paprika to garnish, if you like, and serve immediately.

Cook's Tips
* For young children, the ill, pregnant, or elderly, ensure that the eggs are thoroughly cooked rather than soft/runny.
* You can buy rye bread in most delicatessens, specialty stores and major supermarkets.

Quick and Spicy Pâté with Tuna

> **NUTRITION NOTES** This pâté is a good source of omega-3 fatty acids, vitamins B6 and B12, and selenium.

SERVES 4 Ⓓ Ⓟ Ⓒ (aged over 1 year), Ⓠ Ⓛ

10¹/₂ oz/300 g canned tuna chunks, drained
generous ³/₄ cup lowfat plain yogurt
2 tsp horseradish sauce
juice of ¹/₂ lemon
1 tbsp chopped fresh parsley
pepper
toasted rye bread or whole wheat pita bread, for serving

1 Flake the canned tuna into a bowl. Add all the remaining ingredients and mash together. Season to taste with pepper. Cover and chill in the refrigerator for 1 hour.

2 Serve the pâté with toasted rye bread.

Main Courses—
Fish and Seafood

Our selection of tasty fish and seafood recipes includes several that are not only high in omega-3, but also rich in a variety of other "brain food" nutrients. Whether you are looking for a quick and easy supper or a dinner party dish, there is plenty to choose from. Try to buy the freshest fish you can for maximum taste and best texture.

KEY
Ⓥ Suitable for vegetarians
Ⓓ Ideal for weight control
Ⓟ Suitable for pregnancy
Ⓒ Suitable for children
Ⓠ Quick to prepare and cook
Ⓛ Low cost

Thai Swordfish Kabobs

NUTRITION NOTES These kabobs are a good source of omega-3 fatty acids, l-tyrosine, selenium, vitamin B12, vitamin C, and antioxidants.

SERVES 4 Ⓓ Ⓠ

1 lb 9 oz/700 g swordfish steaks, cut into bite-size chunks
2 red bell peppers, seeded and cut into bite-size squares
1 red onion, cut into bite-size chunks
2 limes
2 garlic cloves, finely chopped
2 tsp chopped fresh ginger
2 red chiles, seeded and finely chopped
1 tsp dried lemongrass
2 tbsp sesame oil
1 handful fresh cilantro leaves

1 Put the swordfish, red bell pepper and onion in a nonmetallic dish. Finely grate the rind (without pith) from one of the limes and add to the dish, then squeeze the juice from both limes and add to the dish along with all the remaining ingredients. Stir well, then cover and let marinate in a cool place for 30 minutes–1 hour, if possible.

2 Preheat the broiler or a gas barbecue to high, or prepare a charcoal barbecue. Thread the swordfish, red bell peppers, and onion alternately onto 4 metal kabob sticks (or wooden kabob sticks, presoaked in cold water for 30 minutes). Cook the kabobs under the broiler or over the barbecue for 8 minutes, turning halfway through and spooning any remaining marinade over as you do so. Serve immediately.

Cook's Tips
* Put the fish in the refrigerator if leaving for more than 30 minutes to marinate.
* The kabobs are great served with rice and a herby side salad.

Variations
* You can choose monkfish, halibut, or other firm-fleshed fish for this recipe. If using any fish other than swordfish, shark, or marlin, this recipe will be suitable for children under 16 and pregnant women.
* Choose mild or hot chiles, according to preference.

Swordfish Steaks with Lemon Dressing

NUTRITION NOTES This dish is a good source of omega-3 fatty acids, l-tyrosine, vitamin B12, selenium, and antioxidants.

SERVES 4 Ⓓ Ⓠ

5 tbsp olive oil, plus extra for brushing
juice of ½ large or 1 small lemon
2 garlic cloves, well crushed
2 tsp finely chopped fresh oregano
2 tbsp chopped fresh parsley
4 swordfish steaks, about 6 oz/175 g each
salt and pepper

1 Put all the ingredients, except the swordfish, with a little salt and pepper to taste, in a screw-top jar and shake well to combine.

2 Preheat a ridged broiler pan over high heat. Pat the swordfish steaks dry with paper towels and lightly brush with oil on both sides. When the broiler pan is very hot, add the swordfish steaks and cook for 2 minutes on each side, or until cooked through but still moist inside.

3 Serve the swordfish immediately, with the lemon dressing drizzled over—shake it again before drizzling.

Cook's Tips
* This dish is good served with new potatoes and green vegetables such as broccoli or asparagus, or a salad.
* Instead of broiling the swordfish, you can simply cook it in a nonstick skillet.
* If you can't find fresh oregano, use 1 teaspoon dried oregano.

Variation
* This recipe also works well with sea bass and halibut. If not using swordfish, marlin, or shark, this recipe is suitable for children under 16 and pregnant women.

Teriyaki Salmon Fillets with Chinese Noodles

NUTRITION NOTES This dish is a good source of omega-3 fatty acids, choline, vitamins B1, B6, B12, selenium, and magnesium.

SERVES 4 Ⓓ Ⓟ Ⓒ Ⓠ Ⓛ

4 salmon fillets, about 7 oz/200 g each

1/2 cup teriyaki marinade

1 shallot, sliced

3/4-inch/2-cm piece fresh ginger, peeled and finely chopped

2 carrots, sliced

4 oz/115 g closed-cup mushrooms, sliced

5 cups vegetable stock

9 oz/250 g dried medium egg noodles

1 cup frozen peas

6 oz/175 g Napa cabbage, shredded

4 scallions, sliced

1 Wipe off any fish scales from the salmon skin. Arrange the salmon fillets, skin-side up, in a dish just large enough to fit them in a single layer. Mix the teriyaki marinade with the shallot and ginger in a small bowl and pour over the salmon. Cover and let marinate in the refrigerator for at least 1 hour, turning the salmon over halfway through the marinating time.

2 Put the carrots, mushrooms, and stock into a large pan. Arrange the salmon, skin-side down, on a shallow baking sheet. Pour the fish marinade into the pan of vegetables and stock and bring to a boil. Reduce the heat, cover, and let simmer for 10 minutes.

3 Meanwhile, preheat the broiler to medium. Cook the salmon under the preheated broiler for 10–15 minutes, depending on the thickness of the fillets, until the flesh turns pink and flakes easily. Remove from the broiler and keep warm.

4 Add the noodles and peas to the stock and return to a boil. Reduce the heat, cover, and let simmer for 5 minutes, or until the noodles are tender. Stir in the Napa cabbage and scallions and heat through for 1 minute.

Tuna Steaks with Catalan Sauce

NUTRITION NOTES This dish is a good source of omega-3 fatty acids, vitamins B6, B12, C, and E, carotenes, and selenium.

SERVES 4 Ⓓ Ⓟ Ⓒ Ⓠ

2 tbsp olive oil, plus extra for brushing

1 onion, chopped

2 red bell peppers, seeded and chopped

1 red chile, seeded and chopped

1 garlic clove, chopped

14 oz/400 g canned chopped tomatoes

dash of white wine vinegar

generous 1/2 cup ground almonds

4 tuna steaks, about 4 1/2 oz/125 g each

salt and pepper

1 Heat the oil in a nonstick skillet over medium-high heat, add the onion and red bell peppers and cook, stirring frequently, for 10 minutes, or until soft. Add the chile and garlic and cook, stirring, for 1 minute. Add the tomatoes and their juice, then bring to a simmer and cook for 15 minutes. Stir in the vinegar.

2 Transfer the tomato mixture to a blender or food processor. Add the ground almonds and blend for 20 seconds, or until smooth. Season with a little salt and pepper to taste, and add a little water if the mixture is too thick to pour.

3 Preheat the broiler to high, or heat a skillet or ridged broiler pan over high heat. Pat the tuna steaks dry with paper towels and lightly brush with oil on both sides. Cook under the preheated broiler or in the very hot skillet or broiler pan for 1 minute on each side to sear, or until cooked to your liking.

4 Serve the tuna steaks immediately on warmed plates, with the sauce spooned around.

Cook's Tip

* Don't overcook tuna, otherwise it will become dry, and don't overblend the sauce, or the almonds will become greasy.

Broiled Salmon with Green Lentils and Caper Sauce

NUTRITION NOTES This dish is rich in omega-3 fatty acids, vitamins B1, B6, B12 and E, folate, and selenium.

SERVES 4 ⒹⓅⒸⓆⓁ

scant 1 cup green lentils

5 tbsp light olive oil

2 tbsp balsamic vinegar

2 scallions or 1 mild shallot, finely chopped

2 garlic cloves, well crushed

2 tsp smooth Dijon mustard

1 heaped tbsp capers, rinsed

1 tbsp chopped fresh dill

4 salmon steaks or fillets, about 5$\frac{1}{2}$ oz/150 g each

salt and pepper

fresh dill sprigs, for garnish

1 Cook the lentils in a saucepan of boiling water for 25 minutes, or until tender.

2 Meanwhile, put all the remaining ingredients, except the salmon, with a little salt and pepper to taste, in a screw-top jar and shake well to combine.

3 When the lentils are cooked, drain, then tip into a bowl and mix in the dressing.

4 Preheat the broiler to high. Cook the salmon steaks under the preheated broiler for 5 minutes, or until cooked through but still moist inside.

5 Serve the salmon steaks immediately on a bed of the dressed lentils, garnished with the dill sprigs.

Cook's Tips

* Buy organic or wild salmon, which tends to have higher levels of the important omega-3 fatty acids.
* This dish is good served with a tomato salad.

Fish and Filo Pie

NUTRITION NOTES This pie is a good source of omega-3 fatty acids, l-tyrosine, choline, vitamin B6, lutein, selenium, zinc, and iron.

SERVES 4 Ⓟ Ⓒ (aged over 1 year), Ⓛ

1 lb 2 oz/500 g mixed fish fillets, such as haddock, monkfish, sea bass, and/or salmon

2 $\frac{1}{2}$ cups skim milk

1 small onion, peeled but kept whole

6 black peppercorns

1 heaped tbsp sauce flour or corn strach

1 tsp smooth Dijon mustard

3$\frac{1}{2}$ oz/100 g cooked peeled shrimp

5$\frac{1}{2}$ oz/150 g cooked baby spinach, well drained

2 hard-cooked eggs, shelled and quartered

1 tbsp chopped fresh parsley

6 sheets filo pastry, thawed if frozen

olive oil, for brushing

salt

1 Preheat the oven to 375°F/190°C.

2 Put the fish fillets in a large saucepan with the milk, onion, and peppercorns. Bring to a simmer and simmer gently for 4–5 minutes, or until the fish is just cooked. Remove the fish with a fish slice and cut into bite-size pieces. Remove the peppercorns.

3 Add the sauce flour to the milk and heat over medium heat, whisking constantly, until the mixture thickens. Stir in the mustard and a little salt to taste. Remove from the heat.

4 Arrange the fish, shrimp, spinach, eggs, and parsley in a baking dish and pour the white sauce evenly over the top.

5 Take the pastry sheets from their pack, then quickly gather each one up into folds and place on the pie, side by side but slightly overlapping, until the dish is covered. Brush the top thoroughly with oil.

6 Bake in the preheated oven for 25 minutes, or until the top is golden. Serve immediately.

Cook's Tips
* Sauce flour is useful, as you don't need any fat to make a white sauce—it is available in most supermarkets.
* If the white sauce seems a little thick—it should be a good pouring consistency—just add some hot water and whisk again.
* Try to include some salmon for its omega-3 fatty acids.
* Serve with a selection of vegetables.

Variation
* You can add 2–3 tablespoons of grated cheddar cheese to the white sauce, if you like.

Salmon Potato Patties with Jalapeño

SERVES 4 ⒟ ⒫ ⒞ ⒬ ⒧

14 oz/400 g potatoes, peeled and cut into medium-size chunks

14 oz/400 g skinless salmon fillet

2 tbsp mayonnaise

1 egg, beaten

dash of skim milk, if needed

2 red jalapeño chiles, seeded and finely chopped

1 small bunch fresh cilantro leaves

all-purpose flour, for dusting

1 tbsp olive oil

salt and pepper

1 Cook the potatoes in a large saucepan of lightly salted boiling water for 15 minutes, or until tender.

2 Meanwhile, lightly poach the salmon fillet in a saucepan of gently simmering water for 5–6 minutes (if in one piece), or until just cooked but still moist. Alternatively, cut into 4 evenly sized pieces and cook in a microwave oven on medium heat for 3 minutes, then turn the pieces around so that the cooked parts are in the center, and cook for an additional 1–2 minutes—the fish should be lightly cooked. Using a fork, flake the flesh into a bowl.

NUTRITION NOTES These patties are a good source of omega-3 fatty acids, B vitamins, vitamin E, and selenium, and also contain vitamin C and antioxidants.

3 Drain the potatoes, then return to the saucepan (if a colander is used to drain) and, while still warm, roughly mash with a fork, adding the mayonnaise, egg, and milk, if needed—the mixture must remain firm, so add only if necessary and only a little. Stir in the chiles, cilantro leaves, and a little salt and pepper to taste, then lightly mix in the salmon flakes.

4 With floured hands, form the mixture into 8 small patties. Heat the oil in a large, nonstick skillet over medium-high heat, then add the patties and cook for 5 minutes on each side, or until golden brown. Carefully remove with a fish slice and serve immediately.

Cook's Tips

* You can use any mild chiles, but they have to be fresh.

* Serve with an avocado salad or a selection of green vegetables.

Trout Parcels with Olives

> **NUTRITION NOTES** These parcels offer a reasonable source of omega-3 fatty acids and a good source of l-tyrosine, magnesium, selenium, vitamins C and E, carotene, and antioxidants.

SERVES 4 ⒹⓅⒸⓆ

4 trout, about 9³/₄ oz/275 g each, cleaned and scaled
2 tbsp olive oil
1 heaped tbsp sun-dried tomato paste
2 beefsteak tomatoes, thickly sliced
12 pitted black olives, halved
1 heaped tbsp chopped fresh flat-leaf parsley or basil
pepper
lemon or lime wedges, for serving

1 Preheat the oven to 350°F/180°C.

2 Lay each fish on an individual sheet of nonstick parchment paper. Mix the oil and sun-dried tomato paste together in a small bowl, then spoon the mixture over the fish.

3 Arrange the tomato slices and olive halves over the top and then scatter over the herbs and season to taste with pepper.

4 Fold up each sheet of parchment paper to enclose the ingredients securely, leaving an air pocket over each fish. Transfer the parcels to a baking sheet and bake in the center of the preheated oven for 20 minutes, or until the fish is cooked through.

5 Serve in the parcels, garnished with lemon or lime wedges.

Variations
* You can use any small to medium whole fish.
* You can use red pesto instead of sun-dried tomato paste.

Baked Sea Bass with White Bean Purée

> **NUTRITION NOTES** This dish is a good source of omega-3 fatty acids, l-tyrosine, vitamins B1, B6, and C, folate, iron, magnesium, selenium, carotene, and antioxidants.

SERVES 4 ⒹⓅⒸⓆ

2 tbsp olive oil
1 tbsp fresh thyme leaves
4 large sea bass fillets, about 6 oz/175 g each
cherry tomatoes on the vine, for serving
salt and pepper

WHITE BEAN PURÉE
3 tbsp olive oil
2 garlic cloves, chopped
1 lb 12 oz/800 g canned cannellini or lima beans, drained and rinsed
juice of 1 lemon
2–3 tbsp water
4 tbsp chopped fresh flat-leaf parsley

1 Preheat the oven to 400°F/200°C. Mix the oil, thyme, and a little salt and pepper to taste together in a small bowl or pitcher. Arrange the sea bass fillets on a baking sheet, then pour over the oil mixture and carefully turn to coat well. Put the tray on the top shelf of the preheated oven and bake for 15 minutes.

2 Meanwhile, make the bean purée. Heat the oil in a saucepan over a medium heat, then add the garlic and cook, stirring, for 1 minute. Add the beans and heat through for 3–4 minutes, then add the lemon juice and a little salt and pepper to taste. Transfer to a blender or food processor, then add the water and blend lightly until you have a purée. Alternatively, mash thoroughly with a fork. Stir the parsley into the purée.

3 Serve the sea bass fillets on top of the warm bean purée with a drizzle of any pan juices. Serve with vine tomatoes.

Cook's Tip
* If the fish fillets are thin, they may cook in less than the specified baking time. Check and remove from the oven after 8–10 minutes if necessary.

Seafood Provençale

NUTRITION NOTES This dish is a good source of vitamins B12 and C, magnesium, zinc, selenium, and antioxidants, and omega-3 fatty acids.

SERVES 4 Ⓓ Ⓟ Ⓒ (aged over 5 years), Ⓠ

2 tbsp olive oil

12 raw scallops, shelled, cleaned, and halved

1 large onion, finely chopped

2 garlic cloves, well crushed

14 oz/400 g canned chopped tomatoes

2 tsp dried Herbes de Provence

²/₃ cup dry white wine

1 mild red chile, seeded and chopped (optional)

5 oz/150 g cooked shelled mussels

7 oz/200 g large cooked, peeled jumbo shrimp

pepper

2 tbsp chopped fresh parsley, for serving

1 Heat the oil in a large skillet over high heat, then add the scallops and cook for 30 seconds on each side to sear. Remove with a fish slice and set aside.

2 Reduce the heat to medium, then add the onion and cook for 8–10 minutes, or until softened and just turning golden.

3 Add the garlic and cook, stirring, for 1 minute, then add the tomatoes and their juice, herbs, wine, chile, if using, and pepper to taste. Bring to a simmer and cook for 20 minutes.

4 Add the mussels and shrimp to the skillet with the scallops and gently simmer for an additional 5 minutes.

5 Serve immediately, sprinkled with the parsley.

Cook's Tips

* Clean mussels by scrubbing or scraping the shells and pulling out any beards attached to the mussels. Discard any opened mussels or mussels with broken shells. Also discard any mussels that remain closed after cooking.

* Shellfish is one of the foods likely to cause an allergic reaction in children, but non-allergic children can eat this soup, or you could substitute other fish for the shellfish.

Spicy Swordfish Fillets

NUTRITION NOTES This dish is an excellent source of omega-3 fatty acids, vitamin B12, selenium, and antioxidants.

SERVES 4 Ⓓ Ⓟ Ⓒ Ⓠ Ⓛ

4 large swordfish fillets, about 7–8 oz/200–225 g each, or 8 small, about 3¹/₂–4¹/₂ oz/100–125 g each

1 tbsp light soy sauce

1 tbsp dry sherry or vermouth

1 tbsp sesame oil

2 scallions, finely chopped

pinch of soft light brown sugar

2 tsp chopped fresh ginger

1 red chile, deseeded and chopped

2 garlic cloves, chopped

1 large handful fresh cilantro leaves

1 Put the swordfish fillets on a heatproof plate that will fit inside a steamer—you may need to cook the fillets in 2 batches if the steamer cannot accommodate a large plate. Put water in the bottom of the steamer and bring to a boil.

2 Meanwhile, mix the remaining ingredients together in a bowl. Spoon the mixture over the swordfish fillets, and put the plate in the steamer, then cover and steam for 4–5 minutes, or until the fish is just cooked.

3 Serve the fish immediately, with the spicy juices spooned over.

Variations

* You can use salmon fillets instead of swordfish fillets.

* Alternatively, you can bake the swordfish fillets in the spice mixture in nonstick parchment paper parcels (if using small fillets, put 2 in each parcel) in the center of the oven preheated to 350°F/180°C for 12 minutes, or until cooked through.

Seafood Paella with Saffron Rice

NUTRITION NOTES This paella is a reasonable source of omega-3 fatty acids and also contains choline, vitamins B6, C, and E, carotene, selenium, zinc, and antioxidants.

SERVES 4 Ⓓ Ⓟ Ⓒ (aged over 5 years)

1 heaped tsp saffron threads

3 ³/₄ cups hot fish or vegetable stock, plus extra if needed

3 tbsp olive oil

14 oz/400 g monkfish fillet, cut into bite-size pieces

1 large Spanish onion, coarsely chopped

2 red bell peppers, seeded and roughly chopped

1 tsp paprika

1 beefsteak tomato, chopped

generous 1 ¹/₃ cups paella or white long-grain rice

1 cups frozen petits pois, thawed

1 lb 2 oz/500 g live mussels, scrubbed and debearded

5¹/₂ oz/150 g (prepared weight) jumbo raw shrimp, peeled and tails left intact

1 Soak the saffron threads in a little of the stock in a pitcher or small bowl for 15 minutes.

2 Meanwhile, heat half the oil in a large skillet or paella pan over high heat, then add the monkfish pieces and cook for 1 minute on each side, or until lightly browned. Remove with a fish slice and set aside.

3 Heat the remaining oil in the skillet or paella pan over a medium-high heat, then add the onion and red bell peppers and cook, stirring, for 5 minutes, or until softened. Add the paprika and tomato and cook, stirring, for 1–2 minutes, then add the rice and stir to coat well.

4 Add the saffron threads and their soaking liquid, the remaining stock, and the petits pois, then stir again and bring to a simmer. Cover and let simmer gently for 30 minutes.

5 Add the mussels and shrimp with the monkfish, mixing in well. Cook for an additional 10 minutes, or until the shrimp are cooked and the mussels have opened, adding a little more stock if needed.

6 Test a mouthful of rice to make sure that it is tender (cook for a little longer if not quite ready), then serve immediately.

Cook's Tips
* Clean mussels by scrubbing or scraping the shells and pulling out any beards attached to the mussels. Discard any opened mussels or mussels with broken shells. Also discard any closed mussels after cooking.
* Shellfish is one of the foods likely to cause an allergic reaction in children, but non-allergic children can eat this soup, or you could substitute other fish for the shellfish.
* Serve with a plain mixed-green side salad.

Variation
* Raw shrimp give a great flavor, but you can use ready-cooked, in which case add them for the last 3 minutes of the cooking time only.

Chili Crab Cakes with Stir-fried Greens

NUTRITION NOTES This dish is a good source of omega-3 fatty acids, zinc, magnesium, vitamin C, and antioxidants, and also a source of choline, vitamin B6, selenium, and iron.

SERVES 4 Ⓓ Ⓟ Ⓒ Ⓠ Ⓛ

12 oz/350 g potatoes, peeled and cut into medium-size chunks
2 tbsp skim milk
14 oz/400 g dressed fresh crabmeat
2 tbsp chopped fresh cilantro
2 hot green chiles, seeded and finely chopped
4 scallions, finely chopped
finely grated rind and juice of 1 lime
2 eggs, beaten
about 3 tbsp all-purpose flour, plus extra for dusting
3 cups slightly stale white or whole wheat breadcrumbs
2 tbsp peanut oil
selection of oriental greens, such as bok choy, mizuna, and
   Chinese cabbage
salt

1 Cook the potatoes in a large saucepan of lightly salted water for 15 minutes, or until tender. Drain, then return to the saucepan (if a colander used to drain) and mash with the milk.

2 Put the mashed potatoes, crabmeat, cilantro, chiles, scallions, lime rind and juice, and half the egg in a large bowl and mix together well with a fork. With floured hands, form the mixture into 8 cakes.

3 Put the flour, remaining egg, and breadcrumbs into 3 separate shallow dishes. Coat each cake first in the flour, then in the egg and finally in the breadcrumbs.

4 Heat half the oil in a large, nonstick skillet over medium-high heat, then add the crab cakes and cook for 4 minutes on each side, or until golden brown. Remove and drain on paper towels.

5 Meanwhile, heat the remaining oil in a separate nonstick skillet or wok over high heat, then add the greens and stir-fry for 2 minutes. Serve immediately with the crab cakes.

Variations
* You could use canned, drained crabmeat, but it is lower in omega-3 fatty acids and may be high in salt.
* Try serving the crab cakes with a chili dipping sauce.

Spicy Shrimp with Cashew Nuts

SERVES 4 Ⓓ Ⓟ Ⓒ (aged over 5 years, because of the salt content), Ⓠ

1 tbsp peanut oil

5¹/₂ oz/150 g snow peas

5¹/₂ oz/150 g baby corn

1 large orange or yellow bell pepper, seeded and thinly sliced

8 scallions, halved lengthwise

2 garlic cloves, well crushed

³/₄-inch/2-cm piece ginger, peeled and finely chopped

2 tbsp teriyaki marinade

3¹/₂ oz/100 g unsalted cashew nuts

14 oz/400 g large cooked peeled jumbo shrimp

1 tbsp sesame oil

1 Heat the peanut oil in a large, nonstick preheated wok or skillet, then add all the vegetables and stir-fry over high heat for 4 minutes, or until almost tender but still with a bite. Add the garlic and ginger and stir-fry for 1 minute.

2 Add the teriyaki marinade, cashew nuts, and shrimp and stir-fry for 2 minutes.

3 Serve immediately, with the sesame oil drizzled over.

Cook's Tips

* Serve with whole wheat noodles or basmati rice.
* If you have time, toast the cashew nuts beforehand: heat a nonstick skillet lightly brushed with peanut oil over medium-high heat, then add the nuts and cook, turning occasionally, for 5 minutes, or until lightly browned.

Variation

* You can vary the vegetables—zucchini slices or broccoli florets work well.

Main Courses—
Vegetarian and Meat

For all meat and poultry lovers, the good news is that you
can eat lean cuts of meat 2–3 times a week without feeling
guilty. Most meats are an excellent source of "brain food"
vitamins and minerals as well as high-quality protein.

Include 1–3 vegetarian meals in your weekly diet (and 2 fish
meals from the previous chapter) for a perfect balance. The
selection of recipes here will help you to achieve just that.

KEY
Ⓥ Suitable for vegetarians
Ⓓ Ideal for weight control
Ⓟ Suitable for pregnancy
Ⓒ Suitable for children
Ⓠ Quick to prepare and cook
Ⓛ Low cost

Warmly Spiced Vegetable Casserole

> **NUTRITION NOTES** This casserole is an excellent source of choline, vitamins B6, C, and E, folate, and carotene, and also a good source of selenium, magnesium, and iron.

SERVES 4 Ⓥ Ⓓ Ⓟ Ⓒ Ⓖ Ⓛ

2 tbsp olive oil

1 large onion, chopped

1 large leek, sliced

2 garlic cloves, chopped

1 small butternut squash, seeded and cubed

2 carrots, sliced

1/2 cup shredded white cabbage

14 oz/400 g canned chopped tomatoes

1/2 cup brown or green lentils

9 oz/250 g frozen fresh soy beans, thawed

1 1/4 cups vegetable stock

1–2 tsp garam masala

salt and pepper

2 tbsp chopped fresh parsley, for garnish

1 Heat the oil in a large, flameproof casserole over medium heat, then add the onion and leek and cook, stirring frequently, for 5 minutes, or until softened. Add the garlic, squash, and carrots and cook, stirring, for 1 minute.

2 Add the cabbage, tomatoes and their juice, lentils, soy beans, and stock, then stir well and bring to a simmer. Cover and gently simmer on the stove for 1 hour. Alternatively, transfer to the oven preheated to 325°F/160°C and cook for 1 hour. Stir halfway through and check that there is still some liquid left in the casserole.

3 Stir in the garam masala and a little salt and pepper to taste 10 minutes before the end of the cooking time. Serve the casserole with the parsley sprinkled over.

Cook's Tips

* You can buy frozen fresh (green) soy beans in packs from the frozen vegetable counter at major supermarkets.
* Garam masala is a mild spice mix containing cumin, cilantro, and other spices. As an alternative, you could use 1 teaspoon ground cumin and 1 teaspoon ground cilantro.

Ratatouille with Poached Eggs

> **NUTRITION NOTES** This dish is an excellent source of choline, vitamins B12, C and E, folate, carotene, and antioxidants.

SERVES 4 Ⓥ Ⓓ Ⓖ Ⓛ

2 tbsp olive oil

1 large Spanish onion, sliced

2 bell peppers, any color, seeded and thinly sliced

2 zucchini, sliced into thin rounds

1 small eggplant, halved lengthwise and thinly sliced

2 garlic cloves, chopped

14 oz/400 g canned, crushed tomatoes with herbs, plus extra if needed

2 tsp smoked paprika

8 small eggs

salt and pepper

1 Heat the oil in a large, lidded, nonstick skillet or shallow, flameproof casserole over medium-high heat, then add the onion and bell peppers and cook, stirring frequently, for 4–5 minutes, or until beginning to soften.

2 Add the zucchini, eggplant, and garlic and cook, stirring, for 2 minutes. Add the tomatoes, most of the paprika, and a little salt and pepper to taste. Stir and bring to a simmer. Reduce the heat to low, then cover and let simmer gently for 45 minutes, adding a little extra tomatoes or water if the mixture begins to look dry.

3 Make 8 wells in the ratatouille and break an egg into each. Re-cover and cook for an additional 10 minutes, or until the egg whites are cooked but the yolks still runny.

4 Serve immediately, garnished with paprika.

Cook's Tip

* Lightly cooked eggs should not be served to young children, the ill, pregnant, or elderly.

Traditional Spanish Frittata with Herb Salad

NUTRITION NOTES This dish is an excellent source of choline, vitamin B12, and folate, and a good source of vitamin E.

SERVES 4 Ⓥ Ⓓ Ⓟ Ⓒ (aged over 1 year), Ⓠ Ⓛ

1 lb 2 oz/500 g salad or waxy new potatoes, peeled and cut
   into ½-inch/1-cm rounds
1 tbsp peanut or light olive oil
2 Spanish onions, thinly sliced
8 eggs
7 oz/200 g mixed salad greens with herbs
4 tbsp olive oil
1 tbsp lemon juice
salt and pepper

1 Cook the potatoes in a large saucepan of boiling water for 5 minutes, or until just tender. Drain and set aside.

2 Heat the peanut oil in a large, nonstick skillet over medium-high heat, then add the onions and cook, stirring frequently, for 10–15 minutes, or until thoroughly softened, and just turning golden. Reduce the heat to medium-low. Arrange the potatoes in the skillet among the onions, spreading everything evenly over the bottom.

3 Put the eggs in a bowl with a little cold water and salt and pepper to taste and beat together. Pour the egg mixture evenly over the vegetables in the skillet. Cook, without stirring, for 5 minutes, or until the underside of the frittata is cooked and golden but the top is still runny. Meanwhile, preheat the broiler to high.

4 Put the skillet under the preheated broiler and cook the frittata for 2 minutes, or until the top is cooked and golden. Meanwhile, toss the salad greens and herbs with the olive oil and lemon juice in a salad bowl.

5 Cut the frittata into 4 wedges and serve with the herb salad.

Cook's Tips
* For young children, the ill, pregnant, or elderly, ensure that the frittata is thoroughly cooked in the center.
* Any leftover frittata is delicious served cold.

Red Bell Pepper Falafel with Hummus Dressing

SERVES 4 Ⓥ Ⓓ Ⓟ Ⓒ Ⓞ Ⓛ

1 lb 12 oz/800 g canned chickpeas, drained and rinsed

2 bottled or canned red bell peppers, drained and finely chopped

2 shallots, very finely chopped

2 garlic cloves, well crushed

2 tbsp chopped fresh cilantro leaves

1 egg, beaten

besam (chickpea) flour, for dusting

1 tbsp olive oil

salt and pepper

HUMMUS DRESSING

1 heaped tbsp hummus

4 tbsp olive oil

1 tbsp lemon juice

2 ripe tomatoes, seeded and finely chopped

NUTRITION NOTES This dish is an excellent source of folate, vitamin E, and iron, and a good source of vitamin C, carotene, and antioxidants.

1 Put the chickpeas in a bowl and mash thoroughly with a fork. Add the red bell peppers, shallots, garlic, cilantro, egg, and a little salt and pepper to taste and mix well.

2 Dust your hands with the besam flour and form the mixture into 8 small patties. Dust the patties with besam flour.

3 Heat the oil in a large, nonstick skillet over medium heat, then add the patties and cook, turning occasionally, for 8 minutes, or until golden brown.

4 Meanwhile, beat all the ingredients for the dressing together in a small bowl.

5 Serve the falafel hot, with the dressing spooned around.

Cook's Tips

* You can buy besam (chickpea) flour from health-food stores or in the health-food section of the supermarket. Alternatively, you can use ordinary all-purpose flour.

* Falafel are great served with a bulgur wheat and cucumber salad.

Sweet Chili Chicken with Creole Rice

SERVES 4 Ⓓ⒫©Ⓛ

8 skinless, boneless chicken thighs, about 3½ oz/100 g each

2 tbsp sweet chili dipping sauce

2 tbsp orange juice

2 garlic cloves, well crushed

salt and pepper

CREOLE RICE

2 ½ cups water

1 ¼ cups white long-grain rice

1 tbsp olive oil

1 large red bell pepper, seeded and finely chopped

1 small onion, finely chopped

1 tsp paprika

14 oz/400 g canned mixed beans, drained and rinsed

1 Put the chicken in a shallow, non-metallic bowl. Mix the chili sauce, orange juice, garlic, and a little salt and pepper to taste together in a small bowl and spoon over the chicken. Using your hands, coat the chicken thighs thoroughly in the marinade. Cover and let marinate in the refrigerator for 1–2 hours.

2 Preheat the oven to 350°F/180°C. Transfer the chicken thighs to a nonstick baking sheet and bake in the preheated oven, turning halfway through, for 25 minutes, or until tender and the juices run clear when a skewer is inserted into the thickest part of the meat.

3 Meanwhile, make the rice. Lightly salt the water and bring to a boil in a saucepan. Add the rice and stir well. Cover, then reduce the heat to low and let simmer, undisturbed, for 15 minutes, or until tender and all the water has been absorbed.

4 While the rice is cooking, heat the oil in a nonstick skillet over medium-high heat. Add the bell pepper and onion and cook, stirring frequently, for 10–15 minutes, or until the onion is thoroughly soft and turning golden, adding the paprika for the last 5 minutes of the cooking time. Stir in the beans and cook for an additional 1 minute.

5 Stir the bean mixture into the rice, then serve immediately with baked chicken.

NUTRITION NOTES This dish is a good source of vitamins B6 and E, folate, and selenium, and is also a source of l-tyrosine, zinc, iron, and vitamins B12 and C.

Cook's Tips

* Check the rice toward the end of the cooking time—if the water has all been absorbed before the rice is tender, add a little more boiling water to the pan and stir with a fork.
* Serve with a green salad.

Lamb Steaks with Tomatoes

NUTRITION NOTES This dish is an excellent source of l-tyrosine, vitamins B6, B12, C and E, iron, zinc, selenium, and antioxidants.

SERVES 4 ⓓ ⓟ ⓒ ⓛ

2 beefsteak tomatoes, cut into thick slices

2 red onions, each cut into 6 wedges

4 large garlic cloves, peeled

1 tsp sea salt

3 tbsp olive oil, plus extra for brushing

1 heaped tsp dried Herbes de Provence

4 lamb steaks, about 6 oz/175 g each

pepper

FOR SERVING

4 whole wheat pita breads

1/3 cup pine nuts, toasted

1 handful fresh basil leaves

generous 3/4 cup thick plain yogurt

1 Preheat the oven to 375°F/190°C. Arrange the tomato slices and onion wedges in a roasting pan. Put the garlic cloves and salt in a mortar and crush to a purée with a pestle. Work in the oil. Spoon the mixture over the vegetables and mix well. Sprinkle over the herbs and season to taste with pepper. Put on the top shelf of the preheated oven and roast for 20 minutes.

2 Meanwhile, lightly brush the lamb steaks with oil. Heat a nonstick skillet over high heat. When very hot, add the lamb steaks and cook for 1 minute on each side to sear.

3 Remove the roasting pan from the oven. Turn the vegetables over, then arrange the lamb steaks on top and spoon over the juices from the corners of the pan, adding a little water if too dry. Return the pan to the oven and roast for an additional 15–20 minutes, or until the vegetables are tender and the lamb is cooked to your liking. Sprinkle the pita breads with water and put them in the oven for the last 1–2 minutes of the cooking time.

4 Scatter the pine nuts and basil over the lamb and vegetables before serving, adding a portion of yogurt and a warmed pita bread to each plate.

Spicy Chicken with Tortilla Wrap

NUTRITION NOTES This dish is an excellent source of vitamins B6, C, and E, carotene, and selenium, and is also a source of folate and antioxidants.

SERVES 4 ⓓ ⓟ ⓒ ⓛ

2 tbsp olive oil, plus extra if needed

juice of 1 lime

2 tsp fajita seasoning

3 skinless, boneless chicken breasts, about 5 1/2 oz/150 g each

1 red onion, thinly sliced

2 yellow bell peppers, seeded and thinly sliced

3 ripe tomatoes, sliced

1 large ripe avocado

4 large tortilla wraps

4 tbsp thick plain yogurt

1 Put the oil, lime juice, and fajita seasoning in a shallow, nonmetallic bowl. Slice the chicken into thin strips, add to the bowl and toss to coat well. Cover and let marinate in a cool place for 30 minutes.

2 Heat a nonstick skillet over high heat, then add the chicken and its marinade, the onion, and yellow bell peppers and cook, stirring, for 3 minutes. Add the tomatoes and cook, stirring, for 2 minutes, adding a little more oil if the skillet seems too dry. Remove from the heat.

3 Peel, then pit and slice the avocado. Warm the wraps according to the package directions. Divide the chicken mixture between the wraps, spooning it into the center of each. Add a quarter of the avocado and a tablespoonful of yogurt to each filling and wrap up.

4 Serve the wraps immediately.

Variations

* You can add a handful of fresh cilantro leaves to the tortillas before wrapping.

* For vegetarians, use firm tofu instead of chicken.

Lamb Kabobs with Greek Salad

NUTRITION NOTES This dish is an excellent source of l-tyrosine, vitamins B6 and B12, iron, and zinc, and a good source of vitamin C, carotene, and antioxidants.

SERVES 4 Ⓓ Ⓟ Ⓒ Ⓛ

1 lb 12 oz/800 g lamb leg fillet, cut into large bite-size cubes
2 tbsp olive oil
juice of 1/2 lemon
2 garlic cloves, very finely chopped
1 tbsp chopped fresh oregano or 1 heaped tsp dried
salt and pepper

GREEK SALAD

3 tomatoes, coarsely chopped
1 small red onion, thinly sliced
3 1/4-inch/8-cm piece cucumber, coarsely chopped
8 romaine lettuce leaves, torn
3 1/2 oz/100 g feta cheese (drained weight), crumbled
8 pitted black olives
olive oil, for drizzling
lemon, for squeezing

1 Put the lamb cubes into a shallow, nonmetallic bowl. Mix the oil, lemon juice, garlic, oregano, and a little salt and pepper to taste together in a small bowl, then spoon over the lamb and turn to coat thoroughly. Cover and let marinate in the refrigerator for 1–2 hours, or preferably overnight.

2 Preheat the broiler to high. Thread the lamb onto 4 metal kabob sticks (or wooden kabob sticks, presoaked in cold water for 30 minutes). Cook the kabobs under the preheated broiler, turning halfway through and spooning over any remaining marinade, for 8–10 minutes, or until the lamb is browned but pink inside.

3 Meanwhile, make the salad. Arrange all the vegetables on serving plates and top with the feta cheese and olives. Drizzle over the oil and add a squeeze of lemon juice. Season with a little salt and pepper to taste. Add a kabob to each plate and serve immediately.

Variation
* You could use pork tenderloin in place of the lamb.

Turkish Lamb Casserole

NUTRITION NOTES This casserole is an excellent source of l-tyrosine, vitamins B6, B12, and C, iron, and zinc, and a good source of carotene, folate, vitamin E, and antioxidants.

SERVES 4 Ⓓ Ⓟ Ⓒ Ⓛ

2 tbsp olive oil
4 lamb shanks, about 10 1/2 oz/300 g each
2 onions, sliced
2 bell peppers, any color, seeded and chopped
2 garlic cloves, well crushed
1 eggplant, cut into small cubes
1/2 tsp paprika
1/2 tsp ground cinnamon
7 oz/200 g cooked chickpeas
14 oz/400 g canned chopped tomatoes
2 tsp mixed dried Mediterranean herbs
scant 1/2 cup lamb or vegetable stock, plus extra if needed
salt and pepper

1 Preheat the oven to 325°F/160°C. Heat half the oil in a large, nonstick skillet over high heat, then add the lamb shanks and cook, turning frequently, for 2–3 minutes, or until browned all over. Transfer to a casserole dish.

2 Heat the remaining oil in the skillet over medium-high heat, then add the onions and bell peppers and cook, stirring frequently, for 10–15 minutes, or until the onions are softened and just turning golden. Add the garlic, eggplant, and spices and cook, stirring constantly, for 1 minute. Add the chickpeas, tomatoes and their juice, herbs, and enough stock to cover the bottom of the skillet by about 3/4 inch/2 cm, then stir well and bring to a simmer. Season with salt and pepper to taste and transfer to a casserole dish.

3 Cover the casserole, then transfer to the middle shelf of the preheated oven and cook for 1 hour. Check after 45 minutes that the casserole is gently bubbling and that there is enough liquid—if it looks rather dry, add a little more stock or boiling water and stir in. If bubbling too much, reduce the oven temperature.

Cook's Tip
* Serve with rice, couscous, or bulgur wheat.

Chili Beef with Avocado Salsa

NUTRITION NOTES This dish is an excellent source of I-tyrosine, vitamins B6, B12, C, and E, folate, iron, and zinc, and is also a good source of carotene.

SERVES 4 ⒟ⓟⒸⓁ

2 tbsp olive oil

1 large onion, finely chopped

2 green bell peppers, seeded and finely chopped

2 garlic cloves, finely chopped

2 tsp hot chili paste or powder, or to taste

14 oz/400 g fresh lean ground beef

14 oz/400 g canned chopped tomatoes with herbs

1 tbsp sun-dried tomato paste

7 oz/200 g canned red kidney beans, drained and rinsed

salt and pepper

AVOCADO SALSA

1 large or 2 small ripe avocados

1 small red onion, finely chopped

juice of 1/2 lime

1 tomato, seeded and finely chopped

1 small handful fresh cilantro leaves

4 tbsp thick plain yogurt

1 Heat the oil in a large, nonstick, lidded skillet over medium-high heat, then add the onion and green bell peppers and cook, stirring frequently, for 10 minutes, or until softened. Add the garlic and cook, stirring, for 1 minute, then add the chili paste and stir again.

2 Push all the vegetables to the side of the skillet, then add the ground beef to the center and cook, breaking it up with a wooden spoon and stirring, for 5 minutes, or until browned all over. Stir the vegetables into the beef.

3 Add the tomatoes and their juice and tomato paste and stir well to combine. Stir in the beans. Bring to a slow simmer, then cover and cook for 1 hour. Add a little salt and pepper to taste.

4 When the chili is nearly cooked, make the salsa. Peel, then pit and chop the avocado. Put in a bowl with the remaining ingredients and stir to combine.

5 Serve the chili hot with the avocado salsa.

Cook's Tips

* Taste the chili towards the end of cooking time, and if it isn't hot enough for you, add a few drops of Tabasco sauce. You can use fresh chiles instead, in which case the amount will depend on the strength of the chile and your own tastes, but 2–4 fresh chiles should suffice. Fresh chiles are milder than dried ones.

* Serve the chili and salsa with baked potatoes, rice, or flatbreads.

Hoisin Beef with Mushrooms

NUTRITION NOTES This dish is an excellent source of l-tyrosine, vitamins B6 and B12, folate, zinc, iron, and antioxidants.

SERVES 4 © (aged over 4 years, because of the salt content), ⓥ Ⓛ
500 g/1 lb 2 oz lean beef steak, such as tenderloin or top round
2 tbsp peanut oil
7 oz/200 g shiitake or chestnut mushrooms
2 zucchini, thinly sliced
2 large garlic cloves, well crushed
2 tsp finely chopped fresh ginger
2 tbsp hoisin sauce
2 tsp sesame oil
about 4 tbsp beef stock

1 Cut the beef into thin strips. Heat half the peanut oil in a large, nonstick skillet or wok over high heat, then add the beef and cook, turning once or twice, for 2 minutes, until browned all over. Remove with a slotted spoon and set aside.

2 Add the remaining peanut oil to the skillet with the mushrooms and zucchini and stir-fry for 3 minutes. Add the garlic and ginger and stir-fry for an additional 1 minute.

3 Return the beef to the skillet, then add the hoisin sauce and the sesame oil and cook, stirring, for 1 minute. Add the stock and stir well.

4 Serve immediately.

Cook's Tip
* This dish is best served with rice or noodles.

Variation
* You can use pork tenderloin instead of the beef.

Beef Satay with Peanut Sauce

NUTRITION NOTES This dish is an excellent source of l-tyrosine, vitamins B12, iron, and zinc, a good source of vitamin E, and a useful source of vitamin C and carotene.

SERVES 4 © (aged over 5 years, because of the nut pieces), ⓥ Ⓛ
1 lb 5 oz/600 g lean beef steak, such as tenderloin or top round, cut into bite-size cubes
2 tbsp light soy sauce
1 heaped tsp Thai seasoning
juice of 1 lime

STIR-FRY
1 tbsp sesame oil
2 carrots, cut into batons
8 scallions, halved lengthwise
2 celery stalks, cut into thin 2½-inch/6-cm lengths

PEANUT SAUCE
3 tbsp chunky peanut butter
2 tbsp canned reduced-fat coconut milk
1 large garlic clove, very well crushed
1 tbsp sweet chili dipping sauce

1 Put the beef in a nonmetallic dish. Mix the soy sauce, seasoning and lime juice in a bowl, then spoon over the beef and turn to coat. Cover and marinate in the refrigerator for 1–3 hours. Presoak 8 small wooden kabob sticks in cold water for 30 minutes.

2 Preheat the broiler to high. Thread the beef onto the kabob sticks and arrange on the broiler rack. Cook for 3 minutes. Turn, then baste with any remaining marinade and cook for an additional 3 minutes.

3 Meanwhile, make the peanut sauce. Combine all the ingredients for the sauce in a small, nonstick saucepan and heat through, stirring occasionally, over low heat. Keep warm.

4 To make the stir-fry, heat the oil in a nonstick skillet or wok over high heat, then add the vegetables and stir-fry for 3–4 minutes.

5 Serve the beef kabobs hot with the sauce and vegetables.

Children's Food

While most of the recipes in this book are suitable for children, this little collection is particularly well received by the majority of kids, from weaning right through to their teens. Even if they say they don't like fish or vegetables, for example, we are confident that they will enjoy these dishes! And of course, each one is rich in foods that will help them to maximize brain power.

For parents who may like to eat with their children, we have included the symbols below in this section.

KEY

Ⓥ Suitable for vegetarians

Ⓓ Ideal for weight control

Ⓟ Suitable for pregnancy

Ⓒ Suitable for children

Ⓠ Quick to prepare and cook

Ⓛ Low cost

Creamy Salmon Pasta

NUTRITION NOTES This pasta dish is a good source of omega-3 fatty acids, vitamins B1, B2, B6, B12, and E, selenium, and magnesium.

SERVES 4 CHILDREN ⒟ⓅⒸⓆⓁ
2¼ cups dried pasta spirals (whole wheat if preferred)
7 oz /200 g broccoli, broken into small florets
9 oz /250 g skinless salmon fillet
scant ½ cup plain yogurt
2 tbsp skim or lowfat milk
4 tbsp freshly grated Parmesan cheese
2 tsp smooth Dijon mustard
pepper
2 tbsp chopped fresh parsley, for garnish

1 Cook the pasta in a large saucepan of lightly salted boiling water for 20 minutes, or according to the package directions, until al dente. Add the broccoli to the saucepan for the last 4 minutes of the cooking time.

2 Meanwhile, lightly poach the salmon fillet in a saucepan of gently simmering water for 4–5 minutes (if in one piece), or until just cooked but still moist. Alternatively, cut into 2–3 evenly sized pieces and cook in a microwave oven on Medium for 2 minutes, then turn the pieces around so that the cooked parts are in the center, and cook for an additional 1 minute, or until just cooked but still moist. Using a fork, flake the flesh into a bowl.

3 Put the yogurt, milk, Parmesan cheese, mustard, and pepper to taste in a separate bowl and beat together.

4 When the pasta and broccoli are cooked, drain and toss with the salmon flakes and the cheese sauce. Serve immediately, garnished with the parsley.

Cook's Tip
* You can put the broccoli in a colander over the pasta to steam, if you prefer.

Variation
* You can also add 1 cup cooked petits pois, if you like.

Real Fish Nuggets

NUTRITION NOTES These nuggets are a good source of vitamins B6 and B12 and selenium, and also a source of iron, zinc, vitamin E, and antioxidants. If salmon is used, it is also a good source of omega-3 fatty acids.

SERVES 4 CHILDREN ⒟ⓅⒸⓆⓁ
14 oz /400 g firm fish fillets, such as monkfish, haddock, cod, hake, or salmon
2 tbsp all-purpose flour
1 tsp mild paprika
2 tsp very finely chopped fresh parsley
1 egg, beaten
1½ cups fresh whole wheat breadcrumbs
1 tbsp light olive oil
salt and pepper

1 Cut the fish fillets into bite-size chunks. Put the flour, paprika, parsley, and a very little salt and pepper to taste in a bowl and mix together.

2 Put the seasoned flour, egg, and breadcrumbs into 3 separate shallow dishes. Coat each nugget first in the flour, then in the egg and finally in the breadcrumbs.

3 Heat the oil in a large, nonstick skillet over medium-high heat, then add the nuggets and cook, turning occasionally, for 7 minutes, or until golden brown all over. Reduce the heat slightly if the nuggets are browning too much, too quickly. Remove and drain on paper towels before serving.

Cook's Tip
* Farmed cod is now available, and is a good, eco-friendly substitute for wild cod.

Variation
* You can alternatively bake the nuggets in the oven, preheated to 375°F /190°C. Gently brush with the oil and bake for 15 minutes, turning occasionally.

Tuna Pasta Casserole

NUTRITION NOTES This pasta bake is an excellent source of omega-3 fatty acids, carotene, vitamins B6 and B12, selenium, magnesium, and l-tyrosine, and is also a source of vitamins C and E.

SERVES 4 CHILDREN ⒟ ⒫ Ⓒ
1 tbsp olive oil
1 large onion, chopped
1 garlic clove, crushed
14 oz /400 g canned chopped tomatoes with herbs
a few fresh basil leaves
2¹/₄ cups dried whole wheat pasta tubes
14 oz /400 g fresh tuna steaks
salt and pepper

CHEESE SAUCE
1 tbsp sauce flour or corn starch
generous 2 cups skim or lowfat milk
1 cup grated sharp cheddar cheese

1 Heat the oil in a large, nonstick skillet over medium heat, then add the onion and garlic and cook, stirring frequently, for 10 minutes, or until the onion is softened. Add the tomatoes and their juice, basil, and a very little salt and pepper to taste. Stir and bring to a simmer. Reduce the heat to low and simmer gently for 20 minutes.

2 Meanwhile, cook the pasta in a large saucepan of lightly salted boiling water for 20 minutes, or according to the package directions, until al dente. Drain and keep warm.

3 While the tomato sauce and pasta are cooking, make the cheese sauce. Put the sauce flour and milk in a nonstick saucepan over medium heat, then bring to a simmer and cook, stirring frequently, for 8 minutes, or until the sauce thickens. Add most of the cheddar cheese and stir well. Preheat the oven to 375°F /190°C.

4 Cut the tuna into small bite-size pieces, then add to the tomato sauce and stir. Let cook for 3 minutes.

5 Tip the pasta into a lasagna dish or a similar, suitably sized ovenproof dish, then pour the tuna and tomato sauce over and combine well. Level the surface, then pour over the cheese sauce. Sprinkle the remaining cheese over the top and bake in the preheated oven for 25 minutes, or until the top is golden and bubbling. Serve immediately.

Cook's Tip
* Sauce flour is a very fine-grade wheat flour widely available in supermarkets. Using it means that you don't need fat to make a smooth white or cheese sauce.

Variation
* You can use salmon instead of the tuna, or even chicken fillets.

Salmon Fish Cakes

NUTRITION NOTES These fish cakes are a good source of omega-3 fatty acids, B vitamins, vitamin E, and selenium, and also contain vitamin C and antioxidants.

SERVES 4 CHILDREN ⓓⓟⓒⓞⓛ

10¹/₂ oz /300 g skinless salmon fillet
10¹/₂ oz /300 g firm mashed potatoes
2 tbsp plain yogurt
1 tbsp chopped fresh parsley
2 tbsp all-purpose flour, plus extra for dusting
1 egg, beaten
1¹/₂ cups fresh whole wheat breadcrumbs
1 tbsp light olive oil
salt and pepper

1 Lightly poach the salmon fillet in a saucepan of gently simmering water for 5 minutes (if in one piece), or until just cooked but still moist. Alternatively, cut into 3–4 evenly sized pieces and cook in a microwave oven on Medium for 2 minutes, then turn the pieces around so that the cooked parts are in the center, and cook for an additional 1–2 minutes—check after 1 minute; the fish should be barely cooked.

2 Using a fork, flake the salmon flesh into a bowl, then add the mashed potatoes, yogurt, parsley, and a very little salt and pepper to taste and mix together thoroughly. With floured hands, form the mixture into 4 cakes.

3 Put the flour, egg, and breadcrumbs into 3 separate shallow dishes. Coat each cake first in the flour, then in the egg and finally in the breadcrumbs.

4 Heat the oil in a large, nonstick skillet over medium-high heat, then add the fish cakes and cook for 5 minutes on each side, or until golden brown. Reduce the heat slightly if the cakes are browning too much, too quickly. Remove and drain on paper towels before serving.

Cook's Tips
* Serve with peas and lightly cooked tomato halves.
* This is a great dish for using up leftover mashed potatoes. If you have leftover boiled potatoes, just reheat in a microwave oven and mash with a little skim milk.

Vegetable Fritters

NUTRITION NOTES These fritters are a good source of vitamins B1, B6 and C, folate, carotene, and magnesium, and are also a source of choline, l-tyrosine, and antioxidants.

SERVES 4 CHILDREN ⓥⓓⓟⓒⓞⓛ

scant 3 cups cooked brown basmati rice
1 cup collard greens or leeks, finely chopped
1 small red bell pepper, seeded and finely chopped
1 cup frozen corn kernels, cooked
2 tbsp grated cheddar or Parmesan cheese
2 small eggs, beaten
2 tbsp all-purpose flour
pinch of salt
2 tbsp light olive oil
pepper

1 Mix all the ingredients, except the oil, together in a bowl, with pepper to taste, to make a loose batter.

2 Heat half the oil in a large, nonstick skillet over medium-high heat. When hot, drop 1 large spoonful of the batter (about one-eighth) into the skillet, followed by an additional 3 large spoonfuls. Cook for 2–3 minutes; or until golden on the underside, then flip over and cook the other side. Remove to a warmed plate covered with paper towels, with a slotted spoon.

3 Heat the remaining oil in the skillet and repeat with the remaining batter.

4 Serve the fritters warm.

Cook's Tip
* This is a good way of getting children to eat some vegetables.

Variations
* You can vary the vegetables used to suit what you have to hand. For example, you could add finely sliced mushrooms, zucchini, eggplant and scallions.
* Add some spices, such as 1 teaspoon of paprika or ground cumin, or 1 tablespoon of chopped fresh herbs, such as parsley.

Veggie Burgers

NUTRITION NOTES These burgers are a good source of vitamins B6 and E, folate, and carotene, and are also a source of choline, selenium, iron, and antioxidants.

SERVES 4 CHILDREN ⓥⒹⓅⒸⓇⓁ
1 onion, coarsely chopped
1 celery stalk, coarsely chopped
1 carrot, coarsely chopped
14 oz/400 g canned mixed beans, drained and rinsed
1 garlic clove, chopped
1 tbsp chopped fresh parsley
1 tbsp tomato paste
1 tbsp light soy sauce
generous ³/₄ cup fresh whole wheat breadcrumbs
1 egg, beaten
1 tbsp peanut or light olive oil

1 Put the onion, celery, and carrot in a blender or food processor and process for 20–30 seconds, or until all the vegetables are very finely chopped.

2 Put the beans in a large bowl and mash thoroughly with a fork. Add the vegetables, garlic, parsley, tomato paste, and soy sauce and mix together thoroughly. Add the breadcrumbs and egg and mix well.

3 Form the mixture into 8 small burgers or 4 large ones.

4 Heat the oil in a large, nonstick skillet over medium-high heat, then add the burgers and cook for 5 minutes, or until the undersides are golden. Turn over and cook for an additional 3–4 minutes. Serve immediately.

Cook's Tip
* Serve the burgers in burger buns or with a small portion of oven fries, with salad greens on the side.

Variations
* You can use all canned chickpeas or lentils, or any combination of canned beans for this recipe.
* Add some chopped, fresh seeded chile for a spicier burger.

Cheesy Pasta Casserole

NUTRITION NOTES This pasta bake is an excellent source of vitamins C, E, B2 and B12, carotene and magnesium.

SERVES 4 CHILDREN ⓥⒹⓅⒸⓁ
2 tbsp olive oil
2 yellow bell peppers, seeded and chopped
1 mild onion, finely chopped
1 small eggplant, chopped
14 oz/400 g canned chopped tomatoes with herbs
1 tbsp tomato paste
2 tbsp hot water, plus extra if needed
pinch of salt
2¹/₄ cups dried whole wheat pasta spirals
1 cup grated cheddar cheese
generous ³/₄ cup slightly stale whole wheat or white breadcrumbs
pepper

1 Heat the oil in a large, nonstick skillet over medium heat, then add the yellow bell peppers, onion, and eggplant and cook, stirring occasionally, for 15 minutes, or until soft.

2 Add the tomatoes and their juice, tomato paste, hot water, salt and pepper to taste to the skillet and stir well. Bring to a simmer and cook for 15 minutes. Stir in a little more water if the mixture is not fairly sloppy. Preheat the oven to 375°F/190°C.

3 Meanwhile, cook the pasta in a large saucepan of lightly salted boiling water for 15 minutes, or according to the package directions, or until al dente. Drain and tip into a suitably sized, shallow ovenproof dish. Add the tomato mixture and mix together well. Spread out evenly in the dish.

4 Mix the cheddar cheese and breadcrumbs together, then sprinkle evenly over the pasta mixture. Bake in the preheated oven for 20–25 minutes, or until the top is golden. Serve immediately.

Variation
* You can add pieces of cooked tuna or chicken to the bake at the end of Step 3, if you like.

Thin-crust Vegetable Pizza

NUTRITION NOTES This pizza is an excellent source of carotene, vitamins B6, B12, and E, selenium, and magnesium, and is also a good source of vitamin C and choline.

SERVES 4 CHILDREN Ⓥ Ⓓ Ⓟ Ⓒ Ⓛ

2 tbsp olive oil

1 sweet potato, peeled and cut into small cubes

1 Spanish onion, finely chopped

1 cup canned chopped tomatoes

1 tbsp sun-dried tomato paste

2 tsp chopped fresh oregano or 1 tsp dried oregano

1 large tomato, thinly sliced

3¹/₂ oz/100 g mozzarella or grated sharp cheddar cheese

PIZZA BASE

³/₄ cup whole wheat flour

generous ³/₄ cup white bread flour, plus extra for dusting

pinch of salt

¹/₂ tsp active dry yeast

²/₃ cup warm water

1 tbsp olive oil, plus extra for brushing and drizzling

1 To make the pizza base, sift the flours and salt together into a bowl and stir in the yeast. Make a well in the center and pour in the water and oil. Mix with a fork to form a soft dough, then knead on a floured counter for 10 minutes, or until smooth. Cover with a damp, clean cloth and set aside in a warm place for 1 hour, or until the dough has doubled in size.

2 Meanwhile, heat half the oil in a nonstick skillet over medium-high heat, then add the sweet potato cubes and cook, stirring occasionally, for 5 minutes, or until softened and golden. Remove with a slotted spoon and set aside. Add the onion and cook, stirring occasionally, for 10 minutes. Add the canned tomatoes and their juice, sun-dried tomato paste and oregano, then stir and simmer for an additional 15 minutes. Let cool.

3 Preheat the oven to 400°F/200°C. Lightly brush a 12-inch/30-cm pizza pan with oil. When the dough is ready, turn it out onto a floured counter, then knock it back and roll out thinly into a 14-inch/35-cm round.

4 Arrange the dough in the prepared pizza pan. Lightly brush with oil and spread the tomato sauce over the top, followed by the sweet potato, the fresh tomato slices, and the mozzarella cheese. Drizzle over a little oil and bake in the preheated oven for 25–30 minutes, or until the top is bubbling and the base is golden at the edges. Serve immediately.

Cook's Tip

* You can save time by using ready-prepared pizza dough or a ready-made pizza dough mix—follow the package directions.

Butternut and Bean Casserole

SERVES 4–6 CHILDREN Ⓓ Ⓟ Ⓒ Ⓛ

2 tbsp olive oil

4 skinless, boneless chicken thighs, about 3¹/₂ oz/100 g each,
  cut into bite-size pieces

1 large onion, sliced

2 leeks, chopped

2 garlic cloves, chopped

1 butternut squash, peeled, seeded, and cut into cubes

2 carrots, diced

14 oz/400 g canned chopped tomatoes and herbs

14 oz/400 g canned mixed beans, drained and rinsed

scant ¹/₂ cup vegetable or chicken stock, plus extra if needed

salt and pepper

> **NUTRITION NOTES** This casserole is an excellent source of choline, vitamins B6, C, and E, folate, selenium, zinc, and carotene, and also a source of iron and antioxidants.

1 Preheat the oven to 325°F/160°C.

2 Heat half the oil in a large, flameproof casserole over high heat, then add the chicken and cook, turning frequently, for 2–3 minutes, or until browned all over. Reduce the heat to medium, then remove the chicken with a slotted spoon and set aside.

3 Add the remaining oil to the casserole, then add the onion and leeks and cook, stirring occasionally, for 10 minutes, or until softened. Add the garlic, squash, and carrots and cook, stirring, for 2 minutes. Add the tomatoes and their juice, beans, and stock, then stir well and bring to a simmer.

4 Cover, then transfer to the preheated oven and cook for 1–1¹/₄ hours, stirring once or twice—if the casserole looks too dry, add a little extra stock. Season with a very little salt and pepper to taste before serving.

Cook's Tips

* You can serve the casserole with green vegetables, such as cabbage, spinach, or broccoli.

* For vegetarians, you can omit the chicken.

Three-color Italian Frittata

NUTRITION NOTES This frittata is an excellent source of choline, vitamins B6, B12, and C, folate, and carotene.

SERVES 4 CHILDREN ⓥⒹⓅ©®Ⓛ

2 tbsp olive oil

2 red bell peppers, seeded and thinly sliced

2 zucchini, thinly sliced

2³/₄ oz /75 g broccoli, cut into mini florets, or frozen petits
   pois, cooked

4 scallions, chopped

2 large tomatoes, seeded and chopped

8 large eggs

3 tbsp freshly grated Parmesan cheese

1 tbsp cold water

salt and pepper

1 handful fresh basil leaves, chopped, for garnishing

1 Heat the oil in a large, nonstick skillet over high heat, then add the red bell peppers, zucchini, and broccoli and cook, stirring, for 3 minutes, or until just softened. Add the scallions and tomatoes and cook, stirring, for 1 minute. Reduce the heat to medium-low. (If using petits pois instead of broccoli, stir in now.)

2 Put the eggs, Parmesan cheese, and water in a bowl with a little salt and pepper to taste and beat together. Pour the egg mixture evenly over the vegetables in the skillet. Cook, without stirring, for 6–8 minutes, or until the underside of the frittata is cooked and golden but the top is still runny. Meanwhile, preheat the broiler to high.

3 Put the skillet under the preheated broiler and cook the frittata for 2 minutes, or until the top is cooked and golden, and it is set all the way through. Cut the frittata into 4 wedges, and scatter with the basil for garnishing.

Cook's Tip

* Serve with a side salad of mixed greens and some crusty bread.

Meatballs with Tomato Sauce

NUTRITION NOTES This dish is an excellent source of l-tyrosine, vitamins B6 and B12, carotene, zinc, and iron, and also a good source of vitamins C and E and antioxidants.

SERVES 4 CHILDREN Ⓓ Ⓟ Ⓒ Ⓠ Ⓛ
3 tbsp olive oil
3 onions, finely chopped
3 garlic cloves, crushed
2 heaped tsp dried mixed herbs or oregano
1 lb/450 g fresh ground beef
1 large egg, beaten
salt and pepper
2–3 tbsp freshly grated Parmesan or mozzarella cheese, for serving

TOMATO SAUCE
14 oz/400 g canned chopped tomatoes
1 tbsp tomato paste
pinch of soft light brown sugar

1 Heat 2 tablespoons of the oil in a saucepan over medium heat, then add the onions and cook, stirring occasionally, for 5 minutes, or until transparent. Add the garlic and cook, stirring, for an additional minute, then stir in the herbs. Transfer half the contents of the saucepan to a bowl and let cool slightly.

2 To make the tomato sauce, add all the sauce ingredients, with a very little salt and pepper to taste, to the saucepan, then stir well and bring to a simmer. Simmer for 20–30 minutes, stirring once or twice, until you have a rich sauce. Meanwhile, stir the ground beef, egg, and a little salt and pepper to taste into the onion mixture in the bowl. Combine thoroughly and then form into 16 small balls.

3 When the tomato sauce is nearly ready, heat the remaining oil in a nonstick skillet over medium-high heat. Add the meatballs and cook, turning a few times, for 5–6 minutes, or until golden on all sides and cooked through. Serve with the tomato sauce, with the cheese sprinkled over.

Cook's Tip
* Serve on a bowl of steaming whole wheat spaghetti or other pasta shapes, or alternatively serve with mashed potatoes or rice.

Beef Chow Mein with Bean Sprouts

NUTRITION NOTES This dish is an excellent source of l-tyrosine, vitamins B6 and B12, carotene, zinc, and iron, and also a source of vitamins C and E, magnesium, and antioxidants.

SERVES 4 CHILDREN Ⓓ Ⓟ Ⓒ Ⓠ Ⓛ
9 oz/250 g dried medium thread egg noodles
2 tbsp light soy sauce
2 tsp superfine sugar
scant ¹/₂ cup beef stock
1 tsp corn starch or sauce flour
2 tbsp peanut oil
12 oz/350 g top round beef steak, cut into thin strips
1 garlic clove, finely chopped
1 onion, thinly sliced
2 carrots, thinly sliced
7 oz/200 g fresh bean sprouts
1 tbsp sesame oil

1 Cook the noodles in a large saucepan of boiling water for 3–4 minutes, or according to the package directions, until just tender. Drain and keep warm.

2 Mix the soy sauce, sugar, stock, and corn starch together in a small bowl.

3 Heat the peanut oil in a preheated wok or large, nonstick skillet over high heat, then add the beef and stir-fry for 2 minutes. Add the garlic, onion, and carrots, and stir-fry for 2–3 minutes.

4 Add the soy sauce mixture and cook, stirring, for 1 minute until the sauce thickens a little, then add the bean sprouts and stir again. Toss the mixture with the noodles and sesame oil in the wok or skillet and serve immediately.

Variation
* You can use chicken or pork instead of beef steak.

Breakfasts and Treats

There is no need to deny yourself or your family some sweet treats—breakfasts and even treats can be a good opportunity to get healthy foods such as fresh and dried fruits, nuts and seeds into everyone's diet. All the recipes in this chapter are easy to make and don't take too long, and are packed with nutrients to help boost your brainpower.

KEY
Ⓥ Suitable for vegetarians
Ⓓ Ideal for weight control
Ⓟ Suitable for pregnancy
Ⓒ Suitable for children
Ⓠ Quick to prepare and cook
Ⓛ Low cost

Yogurt and Strawberry Smoothie

> **NUTRITION NOTES** This smoothie is a good source of vitamins B12 and C, and also a source of antioxidants and l-tyrosine.

SERVES 2 Ⓥ Ⓓ Ⓟ Ⓒ Ⓠ Ⓛ

6 ice cubes
1 small banana, peeled and coarsely chopped
1¹/₃ cups fresh strawberries, hulled and coarsely chopped
²/₃ cup plain yogurt
²/₃ cup lowfat milk
1 tbsp runny honey

1 Put the ice cubes in a blender and process until crushed. Add all the remaining ingredients and blend until smooth.

2 Pour into 2 tall glasses and serve immediately.

Cook's Tip
* This can be served as either a breakfast or a dessert in a glass.

Variation
* You can vary the fresh fruit according to what is available or to taste—for example, try raspberries instead of strawberries.

Oat and Nut Crunch Mix

> **NUTRITION NOTES** This mix is an excellent source of vitamins B1, B6, and E, folate, iron, magnesium, zinc, selenium, and antioxidants, and also a source of l-tyrosine, carotene, and omega-3 fatty acids.

SERVES 8 Ⓥ Ⓓ Ⓟ Ⓒ (aged over 5 years), Ⓠ Ⓛ

peanut oil, for brushing
generous 1 cup rolled oats
2 tbsp pine nuts
scant ¹/₃ cup pistachios or hazelnuts
scant ¹/₃ cup almonds
scant ¹/₃ cup Brazil nuts, coarsely chopped
2 tbsp sunflower seeds
2 tbsp pumpkin seeds
1 tbsp flax seeds
scant ¹/₃ cup dried apricots, chopped
scant ¹/₄ cup golden raisins
1 tsp ground cinnamon

1 Heat a nonstick skillet over medium heat and brush with a little oil. Add the oats and pine nuts and cook, stirring constantly, for 8–10 minutes, or until they smell nutty and look a little golden. Let cool.

2 Transfer the toasted oat mixture to a large bowl, then add all the remaining ingredients and mix together well. Store in a lidded, airtight container in the refrigerator.

Cook's Tips
* The mix will keep for up to 2 weeks in the refrigerator.
* It makes a nice topping for yogurt or fruit, can be stirred into breakfast cereals to make them more nutritious, and is ideal as a between-meal snack.

Fruit Crudités with Chocolate Sauce

NUTRITION NOTES This dish is an excellent source of vitamin C and a good source of iron and antioxidants.

SERVES 4 Ⓥ Ⓓ Ⓟ Ⓒ Ⓞ Ⓛ
7 squares good-quality dark chocolate, at least 60% cocoa solids
12 fresh strawberries
2 fresh pineapple rings
1 orange
1 large banana
4 tbsp lowfat milk, at room temperature

1 Break the chocolate into a heatproof bowl that will fit snugly over a small saucepan on the stove so that when you put 3/4 inch/2 cm water in the saucepan, the bottom of the bowl doesn't touch the water. Set the bowl over the saucepan and heat the water to a slow simmer. Let the chocolate stand, undisturbed, to melt very slowly—this will take about 10 minutes.

2 Meanwhile, prepare the fruit. Hull the strawberries and, if large, halve. Remove the central core from the pineapple rings and cut the flesh into chunks. Peel the orange, and remove all the pith. Cut the flesh into segments. Peel the banana, and cut into 1 1/2-inch/4-cm chunks. Arrange the fruit on a platter.

3 When the chocolate has melted, remove the bowl from the saucepan and stir in the milk. Pour the sauce into a serving bowl and serve with the fruit for dipping.

Variations
* You can use a variety of fruits—try mango, nectarine, or a small orange for a change.
* Alternatively, you can pour the sauce into individual dishes and divide the fruit into 4 portions to serve.

Fresh Fruit Salad with Blueberries

NUTRITION NOTES This fruit salad is an excellent source of vitamin C and antioxidants.

SERVES 4 Ⓥ Ⓓ Ⓟ Ⓒ Ⓞ Ⓛ
2 red-skinned eating apples
1 dessert pear
1 tbsp freshly squeezed lemon juice
2/3 cup red seedless grapes
2 kiwis
2/3 cup fresh blueberries
2/3 cup apple juice

1 Core and slice the apples. Peel, then core and slice the pear. Put the apple and pear slices in a nonmetallic serving bowl, then sprinkle over the lemon juice and toss well.

2 Halve the grapes and add to the bowl. Peel, then halve and slice the kiwis, then add to the bowl with the remaining ingredients. Stir, then cover and chill in the refrigerator for 2–3 hours. Stir once or twice before serving.

Cook's Tip
* Serve with one or two spoonfuls of plain yogurt, or serve as a breakfast with the Oat and Nut Crunch Mix and yogurt.

Walnut and Banana Cake

MAKES ABOUT 12 SLICES Ⓥ Ⓟ Ⓒ (aged over 5 years), Ⓜ Ⓛ

scant 1¹/₂ cups whole wheat flour

1 tsp salt

1 heaped tsp baking powder

1 tsp ground cinnamon

4 ripe bananas

scant ¹/₂ cup peanut oil, plus extra for oiling

2 tbsp unsalted butter, at room temperature

scant 1 cup soft light brown sugar

2 large eggs, beaten

2 cups walnut pieces

NUTRITION NOTES This cake is a good source of vitamins B1 and B6, magnesium, and selenium, and also a source of omega-3 fatty acids, choline, folate, and vitamin E.

1 Preheat the oven to 350°F/180°C. Lightly oil a 2 lb 4-oz/1-kg cake or loaf pan.

2 Sift the flour, salt, baking powder, and cinnamon together into a large bowl, then add the larger particles left in the strainer. Stir thoroughly with a fork.

3 Peel the bananas and mash with a fork. Add to the bowl with all the remaining ingredients, except the nuts. Using an electric hand-held whisk, beat the mixture until smooth. Alternatively, use a wooden spoon. Fold in the walnuts.

4 Spoon the mixture into the prepared pan and level the surface. Bake in the preheated oven for 1–1 ¹/₄ hours, or until a skewer inserted into the center comes out clean. Let cool in the pan for a few minutes, then turn out onto a wire rack to cool completely before serving. Alternatively, the cake can be stored in an airtight pan for up to 5 days.

Cook's Tips

* Make sure that the butter is soft when you add it to the mixture.
* If the mixture isn't a good "dropping" consistency after beating, beat in 1–2 tablespoons water.

Carrot Cake

NUTRITION NOTES This cake is an excellent source of carotene and vitamin E, and also a source of choline, vitamins B1, B6, and B12, folate, and iron.

MAKES ABOUT 12 SLICES Ⓥ Ⓟ © Ⓛ

3 large eggs
1 cup soft light brown sugar
³/₄ cup peanut oil, plus extra for oiling
²/₃ cup white all-purpose flour
scant ²/₃ cup whole wheat flour
2 tsp baking powder
1 heaped tsp ground cinnamon
1 tsp salt
1 tsp vanilla extract
3 carrots, grated
juice of 1 orange
generous ¹/₂ cup golden raisins

1 Preheat the oven to 350°F/180°C. Lightly oil a 2 lb 4-oz/1-kg cake or loaf pan.

2 Beat the eggs in a large bowl, then add the sugar and beat again. Add the oil and beat until well combined, then add all the remaining ingredients and stir until thoroughly mixed.

3 Tip the mixture into the prepared pan and level the surface. Bake in the preheated oven for 1 hour, or until a skewer inserted into the center comes out clean. Let cool in the pan for a few minutes, then turn out onto a wire rack and let cool before serving.

Variations
* You can make a simple frosting by mixing together a generous ³/₄ cup lowfat plain yogurt, 2 tablespoons of confectioners' sugar and the juice of half a lemon.
* You can use raisins or chopped dried apricots instead of the golden raisins, or omit the fruit altogether. You can also use chopped nuts—for those over 5 years only.

Blueberry and Banana Muffins

NUTRITION NOTES These muffins are a good source of vitamins B1, B6, and B12, magnesium, and selenium, and a source of vitamins E and C, folate, and antioxidants.

MAKES 12 Ⓥ Ⓓ Ⓟ Ⓒ Ⓠ Ⓛ

scant $^2/_3$ cup whole wheat flour

1 cup white self-rising flour

1 tsp baking powder

1 tsp ground cinnamon

$^1/_2$ cup soft, light brown superfine sugar

1 cup buttermilk or lowfat milk

1 large egg, beaten

scant $^1/_2$ cup peanut oil

1 large ripe banana, peeled and well mashed

1 $^1/_3$ cups fresh blueberries

1 Preheat the oven to 400°F/200°C. Line a 12-hole muffin pan with paper muffin cases.

2 Sift the flours, baking powder, and cinnamon together into a large bowl, then stir in the sugar.

3 In a separate bowl, mix the buttermilk, egg, oil, and banana together. Add to the dry ingredients and stir until just combined—do not overmix. Stir in the blueberries.

4 Spoon the mixture into the paper cases. Bake in the preheated oven for 20–25 minutes or until risen and golden. Let cool in the pan for a few minutes, then transfer to a wire rack to cool completely. Store in an airtight container—they will keep for 1–2 days.

Cook's Tips
* Make sure that the banana is well mashed until almost liquid.
* Buttermilk is available in supermarkets and health-food stores.

Variation
* You can use other fresh fruit, such as raspberries or blackberries, instead of the blueberries.

Oatmeal, Apple, and Cinnamon Muffins

NUTRITION NOTES These muffins are a source of choline, vitamins B1, B6, B12, and E, folate, magnesium, and selenium.

MAKES 12 Ⓥ Ⓟ Ⓒ Ⓠ Ⓛ

scant 1$^1/_4$ cups whole wheat flour

$^1/_2$ cup fine oatmeal

2 tsp baking powder

generous $^1/_2$ cup soft light brown sugar

2 large eggs

scant 1 cup lowfat milk

scant $^1/_2$ cup peanut oil

1 tsp vanilla extract

1 tsp ground cinnamon

1 large cooking apple

1 Preheat the oven to 350°F/180°C. Line a 12-hole muffin pan with paper muffin cases.

2 Sift the flour, oatmeal, and baking powder together into a large bowl, then add the larger particles left in the strainer. Stir in the sugar. In a separate bowl, beat the eggs, milk, and oil together until well combined. Add to the dry ingredients, along with the vanilla extract and cinnamon, and stir until just combined—do not overmix.

3 Peel, core, and grate the apple, then stir into the mixture. Spoon the mixture into the paper cases and bake in the preheated oven for 20–25 minutes, or until risen and golden brown. Let cool in the pan for a few minutes before serving warm, or transfer to a wire rack to cool completely.

Variation
* You can use $^2/_3$ cup stewed or puréed apple instead of the raw apple.

Chocolate Nut Brownies

NUTRITION NOTES These brownies are a source of choline, iron, omega-3 fatty acids, vitamins B1, B12, and E, folate, and magnesium.

MAKES 16 SQUARES Ⓥ Ⓟ Ⓒ (aged over 5 years), Ⓠ Ⓛ
peanut oil, for oiling
8 squares good-quality dark chocolate, at least 60% cocoa solids
3/4 cup low-cholesterol spread
3 large eggs
1/2 cup superfine sugar
scant 1 1/4 cups self-rising flour
1 cup walnuts or blanched hazelnuts, chopped
scant 1/3 cup milk chocolate chips

1 Preheat the oven to 350°F/180°C. Lightly oil a nonstick, shallow baking sheet about 10 inches/25 cm square.

2 Break the chocolate into a heatproof bowl that will fit snugly over a small saucepan on the stove so that when you put 3/4 inch/2 cm water in the saucepan, the bottom of the bowl doesn't touch the water.

3 Add the spread to the chocolate, then set the bowl over the saucepan and heat the water to a slow simmer. Let the chocolate stand undisturbed, to melt very slowly—this will take about 10 minutes. Remove the bowl from the saucepan and stir well to combine the chocolate and spread.

4 Meanwhile, beat the eggs and sugar together in a bowl until pale cream colored. Stir in the melted chocolate mixture and then the flour, nuts, and chocolate chips. Mix everything together well.

5 Tip the mixture into the prepared baking pan and bake in the preheated oven for 30 minutes, or until the top is set—if the center is still slightly sticky, that will be all the better. Let cool in the pan, then lift out and cut into squares.

Cook's Tip
* Serve with some strained plain yogurt for an indulgent dessert.

Walnut and Seed Bread

NUTRITION NOTES This bread is a good source of vitamins B1 and B6, magnesium, and selenium, and also a source of omega-3 fatty acids, folate, vitamin E, iron, and zinc.

MAKES ABOUT 12 SLICES Ⓥ Ⓓ Ⓟ Ⓒ (aged over 5 years), Ⓛ
1 lb/450 g whole wheat bread flour, plus extra for dusting
scant 1/2 cup oat flour
1 tsp salt
1 tsp soft dark brown sugar
2 tsp active dry yeast
1 1/4 cups walnuts, chopped
2 tbsp pumpkin seeds
1 1/4 cups warm water, plus extra if needed
1 tbsp olive or walnut oil, plus extra for oiling

1 Lightly oil a 2 lb 4-oz/1 kg loaf pan.

2 Tip the flours into a large bowl and sprinkle over the salt, sugar, and yeast, then the walnuts and pumpkin seeds. Combine thoroughly with a fork. Make a well in the center and pour in the water and oil. Mix to form a dough, adding a little more water as necessary.

3 When the dough has come together and the bowl is clean, turn the dough out onto a lightly floured counter and knead for 10 minutes until smooth. Shape to fit the prepared loaf pan. Cover with a clean, damp cloth and let rise in a warm place for about 1 hour, or until almost doubled in size.

4 Meanwhile, preheat the oven to 425°F/220°C. Uncover the dough and bake in the preheated oven for 30 minutes, or until the base of the loaf sounds hollow when tapped with your knuckles. Turn the loaf out and let cool on a wire rack.

Variation
* You can vary the seeds and nuts that you add, but walnuts and pumpkin seeds are particularly good sources of omega-3 fatty acids compared with most other nuts and seeds.

Index